Praise for *Maverick*

"There are two important ambitions at work in this book. The first gives historical context to Thomas Sowell's extraordinary genius. The second shows how his work spawned a new, post-60s conservative consciousness in black America. It looks with openness and courage at the often-awkward encounter between conservatism and racial conflicts. But most of all, this is the inspiring story of one of the greatest American thinkers who has ever lived."

—SHELBY STEELE, senior fellow
at the Hoover Institution and author of *Shame*

"An idea-centered life of the noted economist and political commentator. . . . This will be valuable to students of economics, Black conservatism, and public policy."

—*Kirkus*

MAVERICK

ALSO BY JASON L. RILEY

Let Them In:
The Case for Open Borders

Please Stop Helping Us:
How Liberals Make It Harder
for Blacks to Succeed

False Black Power?

MAVERICK

A BIOGRAPHY OF
THOMAS SOWELL

JASON L. RILEY

BASIC BOOKS

New York

Basic Books
Hachette Book Group
1290 Avenue of the Americas, New York, NY 10104
www.basicbooks.com

Printed in the United States of America

First Edition: May 2021

Published by Basic Books, an imprint of Perseus Books, LLC, a subsidiary of
Hachette Book Group, Inc. The Basic Books name and logo is a trademark
of the Hachette Book Group.

The Hachette Speakers Bureau provides a wide range of authors for speaking events.
To find out more, go to www.hachettespeakersbureau.com or call (866) 376-6591.

The publisher is not responsible for websites (or their content) that are not
owned by the publisher.

Print book interior design by Jeff Williams

Library of Congress Cataloging-in-Publication Data

Names: Riley, Jason (Jason L.), author.
Title: Maverick : a biography of Thomas Sowell / Jason L. Riley.
Description: First edition. | New York : Basic Books, 2021. | Includes
    bibliographical references and index.
Identifiers: LCCN 2021001971 | ISBN 9781541619685 (hardcover) | ISBN
    9781541619692 (epub)
Subjects: LCSH: Sowell, Thomas, 1930- | African American
    intellectuals—Biography. | African American conservatives—Biography. |
    African American economists—Biography. | African Americans—Social
    conditions. | United States—Race relations. | United States—Social
    conditions.
Classification: LCC E185.97.S69 R55 2021 | DDC 330.092 [B]—dc23

LC record available at https://lccn.loc.gov/2021001971

ISBNs: 978-1-5416-1968-5 (hardcover), 978-1-5416-1969-2 (ebook)

LSC-C

Printing 1, 2021

For Emily Celia, Simon Dexter,
and Leah Paige

CONTENTS

INTRODUCTION

"How would you like to be remembered?" asked the interviewer.

The year was 2003, and Thomas Sowell, age seventy-three at the time, had been on a writing tear. During the previous decade he had published eleven books on topics ranging from education and culture to social justice and economic literacy. Unbeknownst to the questioner, and perhaps even to Sowell, the next fifteen years would bring nine more original works, expanded or revised editions of five others, as well as the eighth, ninth, and tenth collections of his newspaper columns and other writings.

Asked earlier in the interview of which titles he was proudest, Sowell didn't hesitate. "As an intellectual achievement," he answered, "I would say *A Conflict of Visons* or *Say's Law*," works on the history of ideas and economic theory. When questioned about the long-term impact of his writings, however, Sowell demurred: "I'm not sure anyone can assess his own work. I certainly wouldn't have the objectivity." Lasting influence is difficult to foresee, he added, citing the twentieth-century Austrian economist Friedrich Hayek, who is best remembered today as a staunch advocate of free markets. "People who never heard of him, who never read a word he wrote, are nevertheless strongly influenced by his ideas on economic liberty. There are think tanks in Australia and Jamaica and South America based on Hayek's work that are now directly reaching the public, who have no idea who the source is." For Sowell, personal notoriety was less important than having tested ideas prevail in policy decisions, regardless of who gets credited. "I'm sure that at least 95% of the people in this country have never heard of me, and that's the way it should be."

So, how would Sowell liked to be remembered? "Oh, heavens," he replied eventually. "I'm not sure I want to be particularly remembered. I would like the ideas that I've put out there to be remembered."[1]

This book is a treatment of Sowell's ideas. It's a selective introduction to a body of work amassed over more than a half-century by one of America's leading social theorists. Sowell's corpus is both wide-ranging and voluminous, and you will not find anything close to a comprehensive appraisal of it in the pages that follow. Rather, the goal of this book is to place what he and others consider his most important observations into context, and then trace the intellectual traditions from which those insights derive and the orthodoxy they often challenge. Nor have I set out to psychoanalyze the author or unpack his personal life in any greater detail than is necessary to illuminate his scholarship and respond to various detractors. For those who want a deeper dive into his background, Sowell has published a memoir, *A Personal Odyssey* (2000), as well as a book of correspondence spanning more than four decades, *A Man of Letters* (2007). He's also offered sketches of his upbringing and family in numerous columns and other semiautobiographical tomes, including *Black Education: Myths and Tragedies* (1972) and *Late-Talking Children* (1997).

True, assessing someone's work while neglecting his personal character entirely is next to impossible and in this case would be a great disservice to the reader. Sowell was born in rural North Carolina in 1930 to a family with no electricity or running hot water. His father died before he was born and his mother, a maid, passed away giving birth to his younger brother a few years later. The orphaned Sowell was taken in by a great aunt, who raised him as her son and hid from him the fact that he was adopted and had a sister and four brothers. The family relocated, first to Charlotte, North Carolina, and later, when Sowell was eight years old, to New York City's Harlem neighborhood, where he was raised thereafter.

A bright student with a tumultuous home life, Sowell was admitted to one of New York's most competitive high schools but dropped out at age sixteen. He left home a year later, after a magistrate labeled him a "wayward minor," and moved into a shelter in the Bronx for homeless boys, where he kept a knife under his pillow at night for protection. He took whatever jobs were available at the time—messenger, laborer—for a black high school dropout with few marketable skills. At one point he was so destitute that the foreman at a machine shop where he worked lent him money to buy food. For a full decade, Sowell received his education from the "school of hard knocks," as he put it; he didn't get around to earning a college degree until he was already in his late twenties and had served in the Marines, where he had attended photography school and taught pistol shooting.

Sowell explains in his memoir that these events from early in his life had a profound impact on his development as a scholar and his subsequent thinking about public policy. "In retrospect, even my misfortunes were in some ways fortunate, for they taught me things that would be hard to understand otherwise, and they presented reality from an angle not given to those, among intellectuals especially, whose careers have followed a more straight-line path in familiar grooves," he writes. "I have lived through experiences which they can only theorize about."[2] This type of experience mattered more to Sowell than abstract theory. His early struggles to make a life for himself meant "daily contact with people who were neither well-educated nor particularly genteel, but who had practical wisdom far beyond what I had," he recalls. "It gave me a lasting respect for the common sense of ordinary people, a factor routinely ignored by the intellectuals among whom I would later make my career. This was a blind spot in much of their social analysis which I did not have to contend with."[3]

In this volume, I draw from those recollections—as well as from interviews I conducted with Sowell's friends and colleagues and from my own conversations with him—to present what I hope is a well-rounded assessment. Nevertheless, this is primarily an intellectual biography, meaning that my focus is on the author's scholarly output, not his life story. And as often as possible, I let Sowell make his arguments in his own voice, since one could hardly improve on it.

The first time I heard his name was in college in the early 1990s. During a discussion about affirmative action, someone remarked that I sounded like Thomas Sowell, to which I responded, "Who's that?" My interlocutor suggested that

I read Sowell's *Civil Rights: Rhetoric or Reality?*, a book published in 1984 to mark the thirtieth anniversary of the US Supreme Court's landmark *Brown v. Board of Education* decision and the twentieth anniversary of the Civil Rights Act of 1964. I fetched a copy from the school library and read it in a single sitting that evening. My response was similar to the novelist Richard Wright's after reading H. L. Mencken for the first time. "I was jarred and shocked by the style, the clear, clean, sweeping sentences," Wright wrote. "Why did he write like that? And how did one write like that? . . . I read on and what amazed me was not what he said but how on earth anyone had the courage to say it."[4]

Sowell's writing is lucid and pithy and confident. He combines wide learning and common sense—and makes it look easy. He avoids sanctimony and sentimentality, even when addressing emotional topics such as race. Unlike many other intellectuals, Sowell has spent most of his career writing for the general public, not the cognoscenti. Technically, he left teaching in the 1970s after stints at Cornell, Amherst, and the University of California at Los Angeles, among other institutions. He has been a scholar-in-residence at the Hoover Institution, a public policy think tank located at Stanford University, since 1980. Even so, through his syndicated newspaper column, which he retired only in 2016 when he was eighty-six, as well as through dozens of serious books written in plainspoken prose, Sowell became for many of his readers the best teacher they ever had.

"When I think of his writing, I think of one word: clarity," said the veteran journalist Fred Barnes, who interviewed Sowell for a television documentary in 2005. "There is nobody in America who writes with greater clarity in columns, in books, in longer essays." Sowell, Barnes continued, essentially had a side career for decades as a full-time journalist, and one of the better ones. "He has written so comprehensively on things like racial bias, whether bias by people or racial bias mandated by governments around the world," Barnes said. "The reporting in some of these books is extraordinary. Given my line of work, I'm always impressed by somebody who does great reporting. He may call it research, but it's brilliant and extensive."[5]

I met Sowell in person for the first time while working at the *Wall Street Journal* in the mid-1990s. On book tours he would pass through New York City and meet with the paper's editorial board. Some years later I traveled to Stanford University to interview him for a *Journal* profile, and we struck up an acquaintance that has endured. These days, younger people are more likely to discover Sowell online. When he turned ninety, on June 30, 2020, he had nearly 550,000 followers on Twitter, which is a remarkable feat for anyone but especially for a person who doesn't use social media. The account, @ThomasSowell, was started in 2009 and is still run by an anonymous fan of Sowell's work. This fan asked me not to use his name, because his fondness for Sowell's ideas might make his politically liberal coworkers uncomfortable. But he did allow that he's a millennial from the Midwest who has never met the author. He began reading Sowell in college and got the idea for the account after hearing Sowell interviewed on Dennis Prager's popular radio program.

"I started the account because I wanted to get his ideas out there to a bigger audience," he told me. Sowell, he continued, "had almost zero social media presence besides someone tweeting out his weekly columns. So I started by sharing the column link and maybe pulling out a few quotes from them. And it was sort of a slow build until maybe 2016." That's when he began posting quotes more frequently, one or two per day, including some from Sowell's past columns and books. And that's the only content the account has ever posted—direct quotations from Sowell's books and columns with no added commentary. Thousands of "likes" and retweets followed. "That's when it really started to get momentum," he said. "In the last few years, the account has been gathering about 100,000 followers a year."

In addition to his Twitter presence, many of Sowell's television appearances over the decades can be found on YouTube. Peter Robinson, a Hoover colleague and host of the online current affairs program *Uncommon Knowledge*, told me his frequent interviews with Sowell are especially popular among people in their twenties and thirties. "Tom is the most appreciated, the most enjoyed, the most requested guest," he said. "The younger the audience, the more they love Tom Sowell."[6]

A younger generation's interest in Sowell is not simply an indication that his views on economics or migration or culture still resonate. As importantly, it suggests an ongoing appetite for his style of policy analysis. The type of thinking that flies under the banner of "wokeness" today was identified more than thirty years ago by Sowell as merely the latest iteration of "social justice" advocacy that political philosophers such as William Godwin were articulating in the eighteenth century. Sowell's adherence to empiricism—to using data-driven evidence to test theories and examine social phenomena—is another distinguishing feature of his scholarship that is never out of date. The intellectual fads that so often animate academics and the media carry little weight with Sowell, who's far more interested in learning the facts and then determining whether they match popular beliefs. While other scholars ask what factors cause poverty, Sowell wants to know what circumstances lead to wealth creation. While others argue over how to explain different economic outcomes among different racial and ethnic groups, Sowell wonders why anyone should expect similar outcomes to begin with. Moreover, he has frequently sought answers to questions that many of his academic peers were too skittish to ask.

In the early 1970s, when Sowell was conducting research on race and intelligence, he was approached at a Ford Foundation conference by Kenneth Clark, the prominent black psychologist whose own research decades earlier had helped civil rights activists successfully challenge segregation laws in public schools. After learning about Sowell's project, Clark privately urged him to discontinue it, fearful that what Sowell might discover would dignify the theories of scholars such as Arthur Jensen, who argued that genetics explained racial differences in mental capability. But Sowell was skeptical of Jensen's theories and wanted to test them. Unlike Clark, he wasn't afraid of what he might find. Nor did Sowell believe there was anything to be gained by shielding people from the reality of their situations. "I did not share Kenneth Clark's fears but, even in the unlikely event that the research ended up confirming Jensen's theory of a racial basis for differences in average IQ, was I supposed to suppress the results?" Sowell asked. He added, "Wherever black people were going, and wherever we wished to go, we had to get there from where we were—which meant we had to know where we were, not where we wished we were or where we wished others to think we were."[7]

These debates are not ancient history. Recent calls to eliminate SAT scores in the college admissions process because blacks and Hispanics, on average, score lower than whites and Asians ultimately are attempts to obscure where these lagging groups, for whatever reasons, currently measure up against others. And efforts to blanket over these discrepancies by no longer measuring them are no less misguided today than when Sowell called them out a half-century ago. Sowell spurned Clark's advice and continued with his research project. He and his colleagues would eventually collect some seventy thousand IQ records from twelve ethnic groups going back fifty years. "The pattern that emerged was that those ethnic groups which were in a similar situation to blacks, half a century ago, had very similar (and sometimes lower) IQs, and as their socioeconomic status rose over the decades, so did their IQs," Sowell later explained. "In a sense, my conclusions go counter to both Jensen and his critics. Both try to find an explanation for a unique black experience, whereas it seems to me that there is little that needs explaining."[8] In Sowell's view, the episode illustrated a broader problem with our discussions about race. "An awful lot of effort goes into maintaining the image of blacks," he told me. "You want to improve the reality, not the image. And sometimes the focus on the image gets in the way."[9]

Sowell may be best known for his writings on racial controversies, but race isn't a topic he initially set out to explore. "I never thought that just because I'm black, that made me an authority on race matters," he said. "I figured there were people who specialize in this stuff and they must know what they're talking about. Then I started reading what they were saying, and so much of it was rubbish. I thought, 'Good heavens, it's time for us amateurs to get into this thing.'"[10]

Sowell is an economist by training, and for him that training started later than it does for most scholars. Never having graduated from high school, his first step after leaving the military was to earn his GED. The GI bill enabled him to enroll in night school at Howard University, the historically black college in Washington, DC, and after completing his freshman year he transferred to Harvard. Choosing economics as a major was an easy call because his best subject in school had always been math. But after taking one course on the history of economic thought, and another on the origins of socialism, Sowell realized that his real fascination was with intellectual history more generally. He wrote his senior thesis on the philosophy of Karl Marx and finally received his undergraduate degree in economics in 1958 at the age of twenty-eight. A year later he obtained a master's degree from Columbia University, and then it was on to the University of Chicago, where he would eventually earn his doctorate in 1968. His dissertation, written under the guidance of future Nobel-winning economists Milton Friedman and George Stigler, was on the history of ideas.

It's no great shock that Sowell's writings on race have garnered the most media coverage. Disputing the rationale behind the Supreme Court's *Brown v. Board of Education* ruling, or questioning whether minority groups benefit more from government intervention than from free-market competition, is bound to earn you greater attention than writing about the history of economic theory or the role of intellectuals in society. But most of Sowell's output is not on race, and *Basic Economics: A Common Sense Guide to the Economy* is his best-selling work. Sowell has written that the "books that made the key differences in my career—*Say's Law*, whose manuscript was crucial to my receiving tenure at U.C.L.A., and *Knowledge and Decisions*, which brought an offer of appointment as Senior Fellow at the Hoover Institution—were both books on non-racial themes." Moreover, his books on racial issues "were not written as an intellectual outlet" but more out of a personal sense of duty, "because there were things I thought needed saying and I knew that other people were reluctant to say them."[11]

Here, his ideas on race and culture will be assessed within the broader framework of his writings on economics, history, and social theory. It is a philosophical framework that has held up astonishingly well over the course of his lengthy career and facilitated a remarkably principled approach to subject after subject, as the following chapters will demonstrate. Books such as *Knowledge and Decisions* (1980), *A Conflict of Visions* (1987), *The Vision of the Anointed* (1995), and *The Quest for Cosmic Justice* (1999) are not about race specifically, but they offer useful insights on where he's coming from in his writings on race as well as on politics, law, education, and other topics. Sowell has opposed affirmative action in hiring and college admissions, for instance, on the grounds that they not only haven't helped the original intended beneficiaries—disadvantaged blacks—but have, in practice, led to slower black progress than we would have seen in the absence of such policies. Yet in his estimation, this negative view of racial preferences is rooted in a much broader analysis of the trade-offs between individual liberty and state intervention:

> Much of the loss of freedom with the growth of big government has been concealed because the direct losses have been suffered by intermediary decision-makers—notably, businessmen—and it is only after the process has gone on for a long time that it becomes blatantly obvious to the public that an employer's loss of freedom in choosing whom to hire is the worker's loss of freedom in getting a job on his merits, that a university's loss of freedom in selecting faculty or students is their children's loss of freedom in seeking admission or in seeking the best minds to be taught by.[12]

Sowell's habit of challenging liberal orthodoxies that are held dear by most of his fellow intellectuals and the mainstream media has led to a good deal of criticism over the decades. This book explores the history and nature of that criticism, why it has been so virulent, and why so much of it comes from black liberals, in particular, who often respond as if any disagreement with the left-wing consensus view is not merely misguided but malevolent. Sowell's adversaries frequently resort to gross distortions of his arguments or ugly character assassination. His motives tend to be questioned more often than the strength of his logic and reasoning. And then there are the outright lies. Sowell has been accused of denying the existence of racial discrimination, of supporting theories of genetic racial inferiority, and of urging other disadvantaged groups to follow in his footsteps or to lift themselves up by their bootstraps—all of which is demonstrably false. He told me that some of these disagreements have been misunderstandings, that his critics are often searching for hidden agendas instead of taking him at his word. That's a mistake, says Sowell, who didn't set out to become an iconoclast. What's driven him from the start was a simple desire to make sense of his surroundings and the wide variety of human behavior on display. "From an early age, I have been concerned with trying to understand the social problems that abound in any society," he wrote in his memoir. "But, once having achieved some sense of understanding of particular issues—a process that sometimes took years—I wanted to share that understanding with others."[13]

Thankfully for the rest of us, Thomas Sowell has a lot to share.

1

CHICAGO-SCHOOLED

"He's a socialist, but he's too smart to
remain one too long."

IN THE SPRING OF 2004, PRINCETON UNIVERSITY HOSTED A
conference in honor of Peter Bauer, the Hungarian-born
London School of Economics scholar who had died two
years earlier at the age of eighty-six. Among economists
working on Third World poverty, Bauer had been something of a renegade. He was skeptical of the view that poor
countries were poor because they were overpopulated or
had been exploited by former colonists. He argued that extensive state control of economic activity was counterproductive. And he was an outspoken critic of the World Bank,
the International Monetary Fund, and other well-meaning
global aid organizations tasked with helping underdeveloped nations improve their living standards.

The conventional thinking in the aftermath of World
War II was that some combination of government central
planning and financial assistance from developed nations
was key to breaking the "vicious cycle of poverty" on
display in parts of Asia, Africa, and Latin America. The

development economist Paul Baran, for example, argued that free-market capitalism may have facilitated prosperity elsewhere in earlier eras, but that it would never work in the Third World. In Baran's view, capitalism itself was now the problem. It was, he said, "in the underdeveloped world that the central, overriding fact of our epoch becomes manifest to the naked eye: the capitalist system, once a mighty engine of economic development, has turned into a no less formidable hurdle to human advancement."[1] The "establishment of a socialist planned economy," he continued, "is an essential, indeed indispensable, condition for the attainment of economic and social progress in underdeveloped countries."[2]

Baran was a highly regarded academic, and such views at the time were well within the mainstream, not only among other US economists but also among their peers internationally. Hiroshi Kitamura, a prominent Japanese development economist at the University of Tokyo, wrote in 1964 that "only planned economic development can hope to achieve a rate of growth that is politically acceptable and capable of commanding popular enthusiasm and support."[3] As Sweden's Gunnar Myrdal, a recipient of the Nobel Prize in Economics, had surmised, the "special advisers to underdeveloped countries who have taken the time and trouble to acquaint themselves with the problem . . . all recommend central planning as the first condition of progress."[4]

But after taking the time and trouble to study the economies of developing nations, Bauer held a rather different view. Having conducted seminal research on trade in West Africa and on the rubber industry in Southeast Asia, he concluded that the conventional wisdom "was in obvious conflict with simple reality." For starters, there was the historical record to consider. "Throughout history, innumerable individuals, families, groups, societies, and countries—both in the West and the Third World—have moved from poverty to prosperity without external donations," he explained. "All developed countries began as underdeveloped. If the notion of the vicious cycle were valid, mankind would still be in the Stone Age at best."[5]

Bauer likewise rejected the idea that the West in general, and free-market capitalism in particular, were ultimately to blame for Third World woes. "Far from the West having caused the poverty in the Third World, contact with the West has been the principal agent of material progress there," he wrote. Just look at the parts of Africa, Asia, Latin America, and the Middle East that had made the most progress: "The materially more advanced societies and regions of the Third World are those with which the West established the most numerous, diversified and extensive contacts."[6] To Bauer, Kitamura's push for more central planning in the developing world was "especially paradoxical since his country"—Japan—"made rapid progress without this policy." The experiences of Hong Kong, Malaysia, Singapore, Taiwan, and South Korea also contradicted Kitamura's assertion. If price controls, protectionism, and foreign-aid packages from industrialized nations eliminated poverty, as development economists the world over insisted, where was the evidence? "There is no empirical or logical basis for the assertion that comprehensive planning is necessary for material progress," wrote Bauer. "It played no part either in the development of the now highly developed countries or in the substantial progress of many of the [less developed countries] that have advanced rapidly since the end of the nineteenth century."[7]

During the 1970s and 1980s, Bauer would expand on his views in lectures, essays, and books, including *Dissent on Development*; *Equality, the Third World, and Economic Delusion*; and *Reality and Rhetoric*. Eventually the conventional thinking in development economics began to bend Bauer's way. The same global aid organizations that had been so hostile to free markets started to acknowledge that there was something to his critique of aid-based development strategies. "Today, many of Lord Bauer's views on aid and development are part of a new conventional wisdom," reported *The Economist* in 2002, shortly before his death. "Even the World Bank admits that creating the right conditions for markets to flourish is the key to economic development, and that until recently much of the money that it has supplied has been badly used."[8]

THOSE ON HAND AT THE PRINCETON EVENT TO HONOR Bauer included the Nobel laureates Amartya Sen and James Buchanan, among other notable scholars, colleagues, friends, and former students. A highlight was the final session of the conference, which featured a conversation on Bauer's legacy between the economists Milton Friedman and Thomas Sowell, both of whom were affiliated with the Hoover Institution, a think tank based at Stanford University. Friedman and Sowell couldn't make the trip east to Princeton, but they had agreed to prerecord a discussion at Hoover for use at the conference.

"The thing that strikes me most about Peter Bauer is how he stuck to his guns through decade after decade—when he was outside the mainstream, all by himself," Sowell began. "And then, by the end of his life, the mainstream had moved over to where he was." Friedman responded that Sowell's own legacy was similar to Bauer's—"You've gone through essentially the same process"—but Sowell demurred, joking that he still had his work cut out. In fact, both Friedman and Sowell had spent a fair amount of time during their long professional careers endeavoring to debunk popular beliefs and to mainstream ideas that had previously been marginalized. In addition to changing the way we think about monetary policy, Friedman had helped pioneer concepts such as Social Security privatization and school vouchers. Sowell's writings questioned the merits of affirmative action policies and the efficacy of trying to advance an ethnic or racial group economically by increasing their political clout.

As their discussion progressed, it became clear that both scholars not only agreed on how Bauer had distinguished himself in the field of development economics but also admired his empirically oriented approach to public policy analysis in general. Put another way, they liked how Bauer thought about the world, and they shared his deep skepticism of fellow intellectuals who were quick to dismiss the experiences and agency of "the masses," or the roles that existing institutions and processes play in how everyday people make decisions in their lives. Friedman noted that Bauer "strongly emphasized that the so-called 'backward people'—the ordinary denizens of India, Malaysia, and Africa—reacted to the same incentives and reacted just about as rationally as the citizens of the more advanced countries."

Like Friedman and Sowell in their own work, Bauer stressed the importance of testing a hypothesis against what could be observed. However plausible a theory may sound, what mattered most was the accuracy of its predictions in the real world. Abstract theories were of little use if they couldn't withstand fact-based scrutiny. What is supposed to occur under a given set of circumstances is less important than what ultimately comes to pass. "It's just amazing," said Sowell, in reference to scholars, such as Gunnar Myrdal, who argued that underdeveloped countries were helpless without large-scale foreign aid and government planning. "I get no sense that Myrdal actually investigated these theories of his and compared them with anything that actually happened." Sowell added, "I myself, of course, started out on the left and believed a lot of this stuff. The one thing that saved me was that I always thought facts mattered. And once you think that facts matter, then of course that's a very different ball game."[9]

BAUER WAS BORN IN HUNGARY, STUDIED ECONOMICS AT THE University of Cambridge in England, and taught for many years at the London School of Economics. His work applied classical economics to questions of Third World development in the British tradition of Adam Smith, John Stuart Mill, and Alfred Marshall. However, Bauer's research and methodology also underscored themes often associated in the United States with the so-called Chicago school of economics, which is one reason his analyses resonated so strongly with Friedman and Sowell. Friedman both attended and taught at the University of Chicago and did more than anyone else to popularize the Chicago school in the second half of the twentieth century. He considered Sowell to be one of his star students. "The word 'genius' is thrown around so much that it's becoming meaningless," said Friedman, "but nevertheless I think Tom Sowell is close to being one."[10]

The University of Chicago has long had one of the top economics programs in the world. As of this writing, its faculty, researchers, and former students have collected thirty Nobel Prizes in Economics, a feat that no rival comes close to matching. Over the decades, the term "Chicago school" has become shorthand for a unique way of thinking about social science. But the reference, when properly used, is not to a "set of tenets or propositions to which all Chicagoans subscribe," as an authoritative essay on the history of the department explains. Rather, it's "an approach to economic research."[11] Not all Chicago economists have identified with this approach, of course, but over time the subset of faculty members who did ultimately came to define the department. And understanding this distinctive application of economic analysis to history, sociology, politics, and other fields of study will undoubtedly lead to a better appreciation of Thomas Sowell's work and the intellectual framework in which he has operated.

When Sowell arrived at the University of Chicago in the fall of 1959 to begin his PhD studies, Milton Friedman had been on the faculty for more than a decade. But Sowell hadn't gone there to study under Friedman, and the University of Chicago hadn't been his first choice. The original plan was to pursue his doctorate at Columbia University, where he had just earned his master's degree, and study under another future Nobel economist, George Stigler. As an undergraduate at Harvard in a course on the history of economic thought taught by Arthur Smithies, Sowell had read an academic article by Stigler on the theories of the classical economist David Ricardo. Sowell was so taken by the subject matter, and so impressed by Stigler's command of it, that he turned his own focus toward the history of ideas and resolved to do his graduate work at Columbia under Stigler's guidance. After Stigler left Columbia in 1958 to join the faculty of the University of Chicago, Sowell followed him there.

Sowell hadn't been a big fan of the intellectual atmosphere at Harvard or Columbia and was looking forward to a change of scenery. At Harvard, "smug assumptions were too often treated as substitutes for evidence or logic," he recalled.[12] There was a tendency "to assume that certain things were so because we bright, good fellows all agreed that it was so." Sowell had little patience for such elitism. His classmates seemed to think they "could rise *above* reasons, and that to me," Sowell said, "was the difference between pride and arrogance, and between the rational and irrational."[13] Nor did he ever quite adjust to the social atmosphere in Cambridge. "I resented attempts by some thoughtless Harvardians to assimilate me, based on the assumption that the supreme honor they could bestow was to allow me to become like them," he said, adding, "I readily accepted all aspects of what Harvard had to offer that seemed worthwhile, and readily rejected all that struck me as nonsense. The fact that I was avidly reading W. E. B. Du Bois did not keep me from Shakespeare or Beethoven. Indeed, I noticed that Du Bois liked Shakespeare and Beethoven—and had attended Harvard."[14]

It would be difficult to exaggerate the severity of the learning curve Sowell faced when he entered college. It's not just that he hadn't been a full-time student in almost a decade. He also was unfamiliar with the basics of the academy to a degree that was startling, but perhaps not unusual for someone who was the first in his family to reach seventh grade. Before transferring to Harvard, he had attended night classes at Howard University. "As an example of my academic naivete at this point, when I heard professors referred to as 'doctor' I thought they were physicians and marveled at their versatility in mastering both medicine and history or medicine and math," he later wrote. "It came as a revelation to me that there was education beyond college, and it was some time before I was clear whether an M.A. was beyond a Ph.D. or vice versa. Certainly, I had no plans to get either."[15]

Sowell's issues with his fellow undergraduates also may have stemmed to some degree from their age differences. He was twenty-five when he entered Harvard, had been on his own since leaving home at seventeen, and had already completed a stint in the Marines. Thus, he was not only older than the typical college freshman but also had significant experience living in the real world. His year at Columbia, a school he described as "a sort of watered-down version of Harvard intellectually," was only a slight improvement. By contrast, the University of Chicago was "itself," he recalled, "and not an imitation of anything." The Chicago economics department was extremely demanding and the vetting was brutal, said Ross Emmett, an authority on the history of the Chicago school of economics. "During that period of time, Harvard took in twenty-five to twenty-seven students and graduated twenty-five of them, whereas Chicago took in seventy students and graduated twenty-five of them."[16] The department also had a reputation for being conservative, and Sowell's political views at the time were, in his words, "still strongly left wing and very much under the influence of Marx."

Nevertheless, he had no qualms about leaving Columbia for Chicago: "I was far more impressed by the fact that we shared similar intellectual values." Graduate economics "is a technical field and not an ideological battleground," he reasoned. "As I came to understand the Chicago views on economic policy, they seemed less and less like any conservatism that I knew about."[17]

THE INTEREST IN KARL MARX HAD STARTED IN SOWELL'S late teens, after he purchased a secondhand set of encyclopedias that included an entry on the German philosopher. It's not hard to contemplate why a black person born during the Great Depression in the Jim Crow South and then raised in urban ghettos might find the precepts of Marxism persuasive. The cruel capitalists, the greedy bourgeoisie, the oppressed masses, the coming revolution that will finally relieve the struggling proletariat from despair—this outlook had a certain appeal to Sowell. "These ideas seemed to explain so much and they explained it in a way to which my grim experience made me very receptive," he later wrote.[18]

Back then, young Tommy was eking out a living as a messenger for Western Union. "When I left home, I had not finished high school and had a number of these low-level jobs," he told me. "It was a trying time. I had always been in school and so on, and this was starting at the very bottom." His job was located in Lower Manhattan, and after work he usually took the subway back up to Harlem, where most of New York City's black population lived. Occasionally, however, Sowell would ride home atop one of the city's double-decker buses and marvel at the shifting urban landscape as he headed north. The bus traveled up 5th Avenue, past the upscale department stores that catered to the wealthy. At 57th Street it would turn left, pass by Carnegie Hall, snake around Columbus Circle, proceed up Broadway, and continue north on Riverside Drive through affluent residential neighborhoods. "And then somewhere around 120th Street, it would go across a viaduct and onto 135th Street, where you had the tenements," he said. "And that's where I got off. The contrast between that and what I'd been seeing most of the trip really baffled me. And Marx seemed to explain it."[19] In his 1985 book on Marxism, Sowell wrote that the philosopher "took the overwhelming complexity of the real world and made the parts fall into place, in a way that was intellectually exhilarating."[20] For a young man in his circumstances who had no alternative vision of the world with which to compare it, Marxism was a revelation.

Sowell would self-identify as a Marxist throughout his twenties. His senior thesis at Harvard was on Marxian economics, and his master's thesis at Columbia was on Marxian business cycle theory. Even his first scholarly publication, in the March 1960 issue of *American Economic Review*, was on the writings of Karl Marx. But like many others who are attracted to Marxist philosophy in their youth, Sowell would abandon it as he became older and more experienced. It helped that he was never a doctrinaire thinker to begin with and kept an open mind. "I read everything across the political spectrum" in those days, he said. "I understood that there were reasons why people have different views, as I see even today, that it's not just a question of being on the side of the angels and against the forces of evil."[21] Even "at the height of my Marxism," he continued, "I read William F. Buckley and Edmund Burke, because I'd gotten in school, particularly in a ninth-grade science class, the idea of evidence, the importance of evidence and the need to test evidence. That was always there."[22]

Perhaps that's what made him such a good fit years later for Chicago, where the importance of thinking empirically wasn't merely stressed but written in stone. The University of Chicago's Social Science Research Building, which housed the economics department, had an edited version of Lord Kelvin's dictum etched over the entrance: "When you cannot measure, your knowledge is meager and unsatisfactory." Theorizing is necessary but insufficient. Data and evidence are needed to verify what we think we know. Sowell had been thinking like a Chicago economist before he ever set foot on campus.

THE CHICAGO SCHOOL OF ECONOMICS THAT PRODUCED Thomas Sowell is most closely associated with Milton Friedman and George Stigler, two of the most influential economists in the second half of the twentieth century. Friedman gained prominence in the 1960s as a ferocious critic of Keynesian economics at a time when the views of British scholar John Maynard Keynes dominated the profession on both sides of the Atlantic. In a 1936 book, *General Theory of Employment, Interest, and Money*, Keynes hypothesized that the Great Depression could be blamed on inadequate demand for labor, goods, and services and that more government spending could prod the economy back to health. Keynesians acknowledged that government spending entailed the risk of inflation, but they insisted that this was tolerable—even a good thing—because it would result in a lower unemployment rate. By their thinking, higher inflation meant fewer people out of work.

Friedman rejected the idea that inflationary government policies were the best way to respond to economic downturns. As a monetarist, he believed that the economy's performance had less to do with government expenditures and more to do with how the money supply was manipulated by central banks. In 1963, Friedman and a coauthor, Anna Schwarz, published *A Monetary History of the United States, 1867–1960*, which argued that the Great Depression was rooted primarily in ill-conceived Federal Reserve policies. Friedman also challenged the notion that there was in fact any trade-off in the long run between unemployment and inflation. Keynesians said that if inflation was high, unemployment would be low, and vice versa. Friedman disagreed, and when, in the 1970s, unemployment and inflation rose simultaneously—a phenomenon known as "stagflation" that Keynesianism couldn't explain—his analysis was validated. "In academia, victory comes when your peers get bigger laughs pointing at your critics than at you," wrote economist Todd Buchholz in reference to the Keynes-Friedman feud. "By the late 1970s, the monetarists moved from being the butt of jokes to the head of the class."[23] In 1976, Friedman claimed the Nobel Prize in Economics "for his achievements in the field of consumption analysis, monetary history and theory, and for the demonstration of the complexity of stabilization policy." It was the first of many Nobels for the Chicago school.

In addition to his scholarly accomplishments, Friedman went to great lengths to simplify economics for public consumption after he retired from teaching in 1977.

He hosted a television series, wrote a magazine column, and lectured widely, and this passion for popularizing the dismal science rubbed off on Sowell. "Milton Friedman was one of the very few intellectuals with both genius and common sense," he wrote in the *Wall Street Journal* after Friedman's death in 2006. "He could express himself at the highest analytical levels to his fellow economists in academic publications and still write popular books such as 'Capitalism and Freedom' and 'Free to Choose,' that could be understood by people who knew nothing about economics. Indeed, his television series, 'Free to Choose,' was readily understandable even by people who don't read books."[24]

Sowell shared Friedman's interest in explaining the discipline to a wider general audience, and, like his mentor, he would go on to make a second career out of it through his books and columns long after he left teaching. Christopher DeMuth, a former president of the American Enterprise Institute and close reader of Sowell's work, told me that in his estimation Sowell was a more effective popularizer of economics and classical liberalism than Friedman was. "For a long period of time, Tom was writing two newspaper columns a week," he said. "He had a beautiful, natural writing style. He was taking something that a hundred people had written about in the past month and writing something that was completely fresh and iconoclastic, with an edge of anger and exasperation to it. I think they were brilliant." DeMuth said that in much of his non-scholarly writing Friedman applied libertarian ideology to one policy issue or another, but that Sowell had more range, and thus could reach more people: "Tom could also get into issues that didn't have anything to do with policy, [issues] that were about society, about the way the people think and talk and argue about matters. He was a more variegated intellectual than Milton, and I think it's an important part of his legacy."[25]

George Stigler influenced economics mainly through his research and scholarly writings rather than through direct communication with the public. But like Friedman, he advocated for greater economic literacy. "Whether one is a conservative or a radical, a protectionist or a free trader, a cosmopolitan or a nationalist, a churchman or a heathen," he wrote, "it is useful to know the causes and consequences of economic phenomena."[26] Stigler's initial focus was intellectual history, the topic of his doctoral thesis and the one that brought him to the attention of Sowell. He was a leading authority on how economic theory had developed from the time of Adam Smith, and his interest in the classical economists never waned. Later, he would conduct groundbreaking research in the field of industrial organization, which deals with how businesses compete with one another, and he would demonstrate how government regulations can lead to inefficiencies that ultimately harm the very consumers they're intended to help. His body of work on the causes and effects of regulation would help win him the Nobel Prize in Economics in 1982.

Stigler also made significant contributions to the study of price theory, or why things cost what they do. Price theory falls within the domain of microeconomics, the branch that attempts to explain the behavior of consumers, firms, and markets on an individual basis. And it was through the teaching and application of microeconomic theory that George Stigler and Milton Friedman distinguished the Chicago school. Other leading institutions at the time, including Harvard and the Massachusetts Institute of Technology, also taught price theory, of course, but it wasn't the focal point of the economics curriculum the way it was at Chicago. Nor did other schools follow the Chicago model in stressing the use of microeconomics to investigate everyday problems in the real world. Instead, most graduate schools emphasized mathematical economics with the goal of developing elegant theories, not testing their worth. J. Daniel Hammond, an economist at Wake Forest University who has studied the Chicago approach to teaching price theory, described it as "more concrete, less abstract; more pragmatic, less speculative; a tool to solve problems rather than a set of problems to be solved, and derived to a greater extent from evidence rather than from abstractions."[27] Friedman taught the price theory course from 1946 to 1963, and Gary Becker, one of his students, said Friedman's emphasis "on applications of theory to the real world set the tone for the department." A strong command of basic price theory was important, said Becker, who later used microeconomics to analyze social issues ranging from marriage to crime and drug addiction. But "the theory was not an end in itself or a way to display pyrotechnics," said Becker. "Rather, the theory became worthwhile only insofar as it helped explain different aspects of the real world."[28]

Friedman himself noted that the key distinction between Chicago under his direction and other schools was "treating economics as a serious subject versus treating it as a branch of mathematics, and treating it as a scientific subject as opposed to an aesthetic subject." To Friedman, "the fundamental difference between Chicago at that time and let's say Harvard, was that at Chicago, economics was a serious subject to be used in discussing real problems, and you could get some knowledge and some answers from it."[29] It was a point he elaborated in a 1974 speech:

> In discussions of economic policy, "Chicago" stands for a belief in the efficacy of the free market as a means of organizing resources, for skepticism about government intervention into economic affairs, and for emphasis on the quantity of money as a key factor in producing inflation. In discussions of economic science, "Chicago" stands for an approach that takes seriously the use of economic theory as a tool for analyzing a startlingly wide range of concrete problems, rather than as an abstract mathematical structure of great beauty but little power; for an approach that insists on the empirical testing of theoretical generalizations and that rejects alike facts without theories and theories without facts.[30]

Although it was Friedman who taught price theory at Chicago, Stigler collaborated closely with him on the contents of the course, even going so far as to help devise exam questions. The two men had first crossed paths as students at Chicago in the 1930s, and a decade later they both worked as professors at the University of Minnesota. Stigler published a textbook on price theory in 1942 and revised it four years later, just as Friedman was to begin teaching his graduate course in the subject at Chicago. Stigler wouldn't join Friedman in Chicago until 1958, but they stayed in close contact in the interim. "Friedman's friendship with Stigler deepened during their year together at Minnesota, and Stigler had a substantial influence on the development of Chicago price theory even in his absence from the Chicago faculty," said Hammond. Through his correspondence with Friedman and through his textbook, from which Friedman drew, Stigler was a teacher "in the shadows for Friedman's students."[31] *The Fortune Encyclopedia of Economics* describes Stigler as "the quintessential empirical economist"; what distinguishes his textbook, *The Theory of Price*, it notes, is "how many principles of economics are illustrated with real data rather than hypothetical examples," a hallmark of the postwar Chicago school: "Probably more than any other economist, Stigler deserves credit for getting economists to look at data and evidence."[32]

FRIEDMAN AND STIGLER WERE HARDLY THE ONLY SCHOLARS of future renown that Sowell was exposed to in his student days, even if he didn't always appreciate it at the time. His professors also included Gary Becker and Friedrich Hayek, who would both win Nobels and profoundly impact Sowell's own scholarship. Becker did pioneering research on the economics of racial bias, and Sowell told me that "anything that dealt with discrimination on my part was within the framework of what Becker had said."[33] Sowell's *Knowledge and Decisions*, which he and other economists count among his best professional work, was inspired by a 1945 academic paper by Hayek on how societies function. Still, there is a case to be made that no one had a greater impact on Sowell's career path than Stigler and Friedman. They were his instructors and his mentors. They served on his dissertation committee and even helped him with material needs. When a problem arose with Sowell's student aid and he contemplated leaving graduate school to find a job, it was Stigler who, without Sowell's knowledge, secured a generous grant for promising academics from the Earhart Foundation. Sowell later said, "[The grant] enabled me to complete the studies that led to my receiving a Ph.D. at the University of Chicago, and to having a career as an economist."[34] And it was Friedman who, years later, brought Sowell to the attention of Stanford University's Hoover Institution, where he became a Senior Fellow in 1980 after he left teaching. Both Friedman and Stigler saw something in Sowell early on that led them to nurture his development as a scholar.

Richard Ware, the longtime head of the Earhart Foundation, recalled receiving the grant request for Sowell. The foundation held Stigler and Friedman in such high regard that the Sowell recommendation was basically rubberstamped. "When he got nominated the letter was very short. I don't know whether Stigler signed it or Friedman or both of them," said Ware. "They nominated him for the fellowship, and they said he's a socialist, but he's too smart to remain one too long. That was the way they put it to the trustees." Given that some nine winners of the Nobel Prize in Economics have been Earhart fellows, the foundation obviously had a nose for talent. "Friedman and Stigler say give him a fellowship, we give him a fellowship," said Ware. "That's the way we did the program, totally on [that] basis. I think Tom should have a Nobel Prize. I'm not sure he'll ever get one."[35]

Sowell would come to view Stigler and Friedman as model intellectuals, not because of any particular conclusions they reached on this or that issue but because of how they went about analyzing problems, presenting their findings, and, when necessary, bucking received wisdom. Stigler, who stood out for both his rigorous thinking and his clear writing, urged his students to test and verify even widely accepted beliefs under the assumption that the conventional wisdom was often wrong. He wrote in his memoir that "the popular acceptance of an idea was little support for its validity."[36] It was an attitude that earned him respect and ebullient praise from colleagues and students alike. "Stigler never deals with a subject which he does not illuminate," wrote Chicago economist Ronald Coase, who would later win a Nobel Prize of his own. "Even those who have reservations about his conclusions will find that a study of his argument has enlarged their understanding of the problem being discussed."[37] Another economist, Jacob Mincer, said, of Stigler's writings, "Almost any sample of his prose shows a tasteful and elegant literary style and an ability, rare among practitioners of the 'dismal science,' to combine wit with wisdom."[38]

Sowell was impressed with how Stigler nudged students to reach their own conclusions while teaching them how to get there. He "jumped on no bandwagon, beat no drum for causes, created no personal cult," wrote Sowell. "He did the work of a scholar and a teacher—both superbly—and found that sufficient. If you wanted to learn, and above all wanted to learn how to think—how to avoid vague words, fuzzy thoughts or maudlin sentiments that cloud over reality—then Stigler was your man."[39] In a condolence letter to one of Stigler's children following Stigler's death in 1991, Sowell said that his former mentor "had a profound influence on my life and career," noting, "He gave me great amounts of his time, by mail as well as when I was in residence."[40] In an essay on his experience as a student of Stigler's, Sowell added, "What Stigler really taught, whether the course was industrial organization or the history of economic thought, was intellectual integrity, analytical rigor, respect for evidence—and skepticism toward the fashions and enthusiasms that come and go."[41] These are the standards that a future Professor Sowell would aspire to while teaching economics at various schools in the 1960s and 1970s as well as in his scholarship in the decades that followed.

In Friedman, Sowell observed many of the same admirable qualities, including the expectation that students would meet high academic demands or suffer the consequences. Friedman's graduate price theory course was mandatory and notoriously difficult. In 1959, the year Sowell arrived at Chicago, Friedman passed just eight of the seventeen students who took his written examination. According to Friedman biographer Lanny Ebenstein, the course was used to "screen out graduate students who did not measure up to departmental standards." Chicago's economics department at the time, said Ebenstein, "followed a relatively liberal policy with respect to admission, with the thought that many students would drop out in the first year or so."[42] Sowell did well, it turned out, and Friedman congratulated him for receiving a B in a class where no one had received an A.[43] The experience was grueling, but in hindsight Sowell appreciated how Friedman had challenged him and his fellow classmates. He described his former professor as not only a "great economist" with a "polished classroom performance" but also a "wonderful human being, especially outside the classroom." Friedman "forced you to confront your own sloppy thinking," said Sowell. "There is nothing more important as a teacher."[44]

Other star pupils shared Sowell's view of Friedman. Robert Lucas, who studied under Friedman in the early 1960s and went on to receive a Nobel Prize in Economics in 1995, also fondly recalled him as a tough teacher intent on sharpening the critical thinking skills of his students. "The quality of discussions in Friedman's classes was unique in my experience," said Lucas. These discussions often were structured as debates between the professor and the students, and what Lucas said he feared most during class was "the exposure of my confusion next to Friedman's quickness and clarity. He would engage a particular student in a dialogue, and once engaged no escape . . . was possible. Exit lines like 'Well, I'll have to think about it' were no use. 'Let's think about it now,' Friedman would say."[45]

As a college professor, Sowell would adopt a somewhat similar approach toward his own students. He taught mainly through discussion rather than by lecture or from a textbook. He wasn't interested in merely testing the recitation skills of students or their ability to memorize facts. "My teaching was directed toward getting the student to think," he explained. "The reading assignments often contained conflicting analysis of a given economic problem. Some students responded to this, but others found it very disconcerting."[46] Sowell's fellow faculty members sometimes found it disconcerting as well, and he had repeated run-ins with colleagues at Howard, Cornell, the University of California at Los Angeles (UCLA), and elsewhere over his tough grading and refusal to compromise. Gerald O'Driscoll, a monetary policy expert at the Cato Institute who studied under Sowell at UCLA in the early 1970s, recalled him as a stern but fair suffer-no-fools type. After

O'Driscoll submitted his final paper for a graduate seminar on the history of economic thought, Sowell called him into his office and said, "Well, yours was by far the best paper in the class, but that's not a very high standard."[47]

Even students on campus who had not taken Sowell's classes still knew about him through word of mouth. John Cogan, an economist at Stanford and a colleague of Sowell's at the Hoover Institution, was never one of his students but matriculated at UCLA when Sowell was on the faculty. "Tom had quite a reputation," Cogan remembered. "A few of my fellow graduate students were [teaching assistants] for him and told me how Tom was very, very demanding." Cogan said he and others found Sowell's attitude all the more remarkable given the general atmosphere on college campuses at the time. "It was UCLA. It was Vietnam. It was lax standards," he said. "We had big demonstrations on campus, classes were being canceled. Students were getting credits for doing antiwar demonstrations and the like. My recollection of Tom was very high standards. No nonsense in the classroom. You're here to learn and I'm here to teach you."[48]

In addition to Stigler and Friedman's impressive classroom demeanor, Sowell also noticed how they conducted themselves as public intellectuals. Stigler, for all his demonstrated brilliance in his own field of study, didn't assume that this made him an authority on matters outside of his expertise. He had a certain humility about his limitations as an "expert." He knew what he did not know, in other words, and this self-awareness struck a chord with his former student. Sowell sometimes quoted Stigler's remark about celebrated scholars who "issue stern ultimata to the public on almost a monthly basis, and sometimes on no other basis."[49] It does not follow that an authority in one area should automatically be taken seriously in other areas. And intellectuals who pretend otherwise, argued Stigler, risk doing a great disservice to society. "A full collection of public statements signed by laureates whose work gave them not even professional acquaintance with the problem addressed by the statement would be a very large and somewhat depressing collection," Stigler once said in reference to some of his fellow Nobel Prize winners.[50]

Sowell shared this skepticism of blindly deferring to the intelligentsia on policy matters. He would go on to write extensively about the nature and role of intellectuals and the damaging ways they can influence public policy while "paying no price for being wrong." In Sowell's view, the results have been at least as depressing as Stigler anticipated. Specific examples include the philosopher Bertrand Russell's calls for British disarmament in the 1930s; the biologist Paul Ehrlich's scaremongering about "overpopulation" in the 1960s; and social reformer Jacob Riis's advocacy of slum-clearance programs displacing low-income blacks, which led to the construction of public housing projects that later became such social catastrophes that they had to be demolished using explosives.

More broadly troublesome, argued Sowell, has been the way in which some intellectuals have addressed issues such as social inequality, where they depict more prosperous groups as the cause of other groups being less prosperous. "Intellectuals have romanticized cultures that have left people mired in poverty, ignorance, violence, disease and chaos, while trashing cultures that have led the world in prosperity, education, medical advances and law and order," he wrote in *Intellectuals and Society*. "Intellectuals give people who have the handicap of poverty the further handicap of a sense of victimhood. They have encouraged the poor to believe their poverty is caused by the rich—a message which may be a passing annoyance to the rich but a lasting handicap to the poor, who may see less need to make fundamental changes to their own lives that could lift themselves up, instead of focusing their efforts on dragging others down."[51] But whether Sowell was writing about intellectual history, income disparities, or some other subject, he utilized a framework of analysis that defined the Chicago school under Milton Friedman and George Stigler.

IN THE DECADES AFTER HE LEFT CHICAGO, SOWELL'S CRITics would use his affiliation with Stigler and Friedman against him. In an effort to cast Sowell as incapable of thinking for himself, these critics would dismiss him as "the black Milton Friedman" or "an apostle" of the "white conservative economists" he studied under.[52] The reality is that Sowell's admiration for his former instructors didn't make him their intellectual clone, and there was no expectation on their part that it would. As a professor, Friedman "did not attempt to convert students to his political views," wrote Sowell. "I made no secret of the fact that I was a Marxist when I was a student in Professor Friedman's course, but he made no effort to change my views. He once said that anybody who was easily converted was not worth converting."[53] Stigler, as another former student pointed out, was much the same: "If you look at three of his well-known students, Mark Blaug, Sam Peltzman and Thomas Sowell, their common denominator is a clear sense of self-direction and self-confidence. They were all capable of standing up to Stigler, of giving as good as they got."[54]

The economist Arnold Harberger, who earned his doctorate from the University of Chicago in 1950 and taught there from 1953 to 1983, said that while the Chicago school certainly stressed the role of market forces in explaining economic behavior, Friedman and other professors weren't in the habit of dragging their personal politics into the classroom:

> Milton Friedman taught for many years at Chicago, but he didn't teach *Free to Choose*; he taught *A Monetary History of the United States*. And the rest of us, in our classes, were not teaching ideology . . . but rather economics as a science, so our vision— certainly my own vision, which I believe is shared by nearly all or all of my colleagues at Chicago—is that the forces of the market are just that: They are forces; they are like the wind and the tides; they are things that if you want to try to ignore them, you ignore them at your peril, and if you understand that they are there, working their way, if you find a way of ordering your life that is compatible with these forces, indeed which harnesses these forces to the benefit of your society, that's the way to go.[55]

If Sowell was his puppet, it was also lost on Friedman, who wrote that one of Sowell's "qualities" was his "stubbornness—at once exasperating when he disagrees with you and yet fundamental to his scholarly achievements.

He has a mind of his own, insists on making it up for himself, and on getting the evidence necessary to form a valid judgment." Friedman added that this quality, "which we call persistence in ourselves, stubbornness in someone we are fond of, obstinacy in still others—explains the extraordinary range of evidence he has assembled in the whole series of books and articles that he has written on the subject of minorities."[56] The charge that Sowell didn't arrive at conclusions on his own likewise would have struck Stigler as absurd. The professor and student crossed swords in class and argued vehemently over Sowell's doctoral dissertation—on the theories of the classical economist Jean-Baptiste Say—to the point where Stigler offered to step aside as thesis adviser, since, as he told Sowell, "we seldom see eye to eye."[57]

As I will demonstrate in the chapters that follow, Sowell's go-it-alone attitude not only predates his Chicago days but also defines his entire career, spanning everything from his scholarship on economic history to his writings on social theory and civil rights activism. When the Supreme Court ruled in 1954 that racially segregated public schools were unconstitutional, Sowell was still in night school at Howard University. During a class discussion on the day of the landmark decision, he and everyone else in attendance agreed that the court had made the right call. However, Sowell was alone in expressing skepticism that racial integration in and of itself "was going to lead to some magic solution to problems of race and poverty," which was the consensus view among his classmates.[58] As he later explained, "I saw the obstacles to the advancement of blacks as involving more than discrimination by whites."[59]

Given this criticism of Sowell as a mouthpiece for white conservative intellectuals, it's perhaps ironic that the academics who most endeared themselves to him were his black mentors at Howard, not his white mentors at Chicago. He described Marie Gadsden, an English professor, and Sterling Brown, an accomplished poet who taught a writing course, as his "two idols" at Howard, "and both remained so for the rest of my life." Gadsden, he said, "was my most important confidante, and her wise words helped me through many tough times in my personal life, as well as my professional career. She encouraged my work, celebrated my advancement and, where necessary, criticized my shortcomings. All of it helped me."[60] Gadsden and Brown both wrote strong recommendations for Sowell when he transferred to Harvard. And Brown, who "understood the pitfalls of a victim mentality," told Sowell, on the eve of Sowell's departure to Cambridge, "Don't come back here and tell me you didn't make it 'cause white folks were mean." Sowell would recall years later that it "was the best advice I could have gotten."[61]

According to Sowell, he didn't abandon socialism because he was bamboozled by his Chicago professors. Rather, what ultimately began his drift to the political right was a summer job at the US Department of Labor in Washington in the summer of 1960:

> The job paid more than I had ever made before, enabling me to enjoy a few amenities of life. Inadvertently, it also played a role as a turning point in my ideological orientation. After a year at the University of Chicago, including a course from Milton Friedman, I remained as much of a Marxist as I had been

before arriving. However, the experience of seeing government at work from the inside and at a professional level started me to rethinking the whole notion of government as a potentially benevolent force in the economy and society. From there on, as I learned more and more from both experience and research, my adherence to the visions and doctrines of the left began to erode rapidly with the passage of time.[62]

At the Labor Department, Sowell was tasked with analyzing the sugar industry in Puerto Rico, where the US government ran a program that set minimum wages for workers. He noticed that over a certain period, as the minimum wage had been raised, employment had fallen. At the time, he was a supporter of minimum-wage laws, out of a belief that they helped the poor earn a decent living. But faced with the facts, he started to wonder whether minimum-wage laws were pricing people out of jobs. He also noticed that his coworkers, the department's permanent staff, didn't much care either way. "It forced me to realize that government agencies have their own self-interest to look after, regardless of those for whom a program has been set up," he wrote. "Administration of the minimum wage law was a major part of the Labor Department's budget and employed a significant fraction of all the people who worked there. Whether or not minimum wages benefited workers may have been my overriding question, but it was clearly not theirs." It was this realization, not a lecture at the University of Chicago, that made him "want to rethink the larger question of the role of government in general," he recalled. "The more other government programs I looked into, over the years, the harder I found it to believe that they were a net benefit to society."[63]

Sowell came to his free-market beliefs by way of reflection and observation. But then, so did Friedman and Stigler, who both spoke of having liberal political inclinations in their student days. Sowell's readers often express surprise when they discover that he started out as a Marxist, but Sowell told me he suspected that at least half his colleagues at the conservative Hoover Institution were also on the left in their twenties.[64] And that's certainly true of any number of notable black dissident thinkers, from Clarence Thomas and Shelby Steele to Walter Williams, Glenn Loury, and Robert Woodson, who have faced regular attacks from black liberals and other critics often far more interested in questioning their motives than in addressing their arguments. Yet what distinguishes Sowell even among other black scholars, and what will be explored in the chapters that follow, is how his scholarship advances classical liberal concepts far beyond the realm of race.

2

A MAN ALONE

"It isn't fashionable to say this, and it certainly isn't pleasant, but truth does not depend on these considerations."

OVER THE DECADES, THOMAS SOWELL HAD OFFERED sketches of his personal life in numerous columns and several books, including *Black Education: Myths and Tragedies* (1972) and *Late-Talking Children* (1997). But it wasn't until the year 2000, at the age of seventy, that he finally published his memoir, *A Personal Odyssey*. The book guides us through his childhood, his military stint during the Korean War, and his days as a college student. He writes about his first marriage, the birth of his two children, a subsequent divorce, and meeting his second wife, Mary. He describes his repeated attempts to establish himself as a professor of economics at various institutions and explains why he ultimately settled on a nonteaching post at Stanford University's Hoover Institution, where he pursued a career in research and writing, even though his first love had been classroom instruction. Sowell's superb storytelling skills are on display in *A Personal Odyssey*, and the vignettes are both interesting and insightful. Still, it is not a full-fledged autobiography, and the reader is kept at a certain remove. Those who were looking for more introspection from Sowell had to wait until he published his book of correspondence, *A Man of Letters*, in 2007.

It turned out that Sowell was a prolific letter-writer, particularly in his younger years, and even kept carbon copies of his own missives. Beginning in 1960, *A Man of Letters* covers more than forty years of these communications with family, friends, colleagues, and public figures. And in them we can see that the attributes that would eventually come to identify Sowell's writing—the directness, the wit, the swagger, the contrarianism—were already apparent at a very early date. *A Man of Letters* is particularly useful in assessing Sowell's ideas because the letters are less guarded than his memoir. We get revealing glimpses of the character and thinking of a young man in the process of developing critiques of liberalism, government solutions, and other issues that he would not fully address in some cases until much later in his life.

In 1960, after the chairman of the economics department at Howard University approached him about a teaching job, Sowell wrote to a friend that the man "seemed genuinely unable to reconcile my going to [the more conservative University of] Chicago with my coming from liberal Harvard. I don't think it really occurred to him that I have a mind of my own and did not consider myself a 'product' of either institution."[1] What's striking about the encounter is that it demonstrates just how long people have been questioning Sowell's motives and challenging his ability to think for himself. Throughout his career he would be accused by detractors of consciously echoing the views of others or adopting certain positions merely to curry favor or "serve the interests of whites in power."[2] But his letters provide compelling evidence of an autonomy that long predates his life as a public intellectual. And this is especially true with regard to his views on racial matters.

SOWELL INITIALLY WAS OPTIMISTIC ABOUT THE DIRECTION of the civil rights movement. He had been born into an extremely poor family in rural Gastonia, North Carolina, during the Great Depression and raised in a New York City ghetto in the 1940s. Like many other blacks of that time and in those places, his family was uneducated. The men mostly worked as laborers or in the service sector, and the women typically were domestics. Racist laws had reduced opportunities for black Americans and thus limited their upward mobility. Sowell had attended segregated schools and had lived in segregated cities. He'd been turned away from restaurants and housing because of his skin color. He'd felt the pain and humiliation of racism firsthand throughout his life. He needed no lectures from anyone on the evils of Jim Crow.

Sowell lived in Washington in the early 1950s and worked as a government clerk. A longtime hobbyist photographer, he would sometimes wander around the city with a camera and take pictures in his spare time. "I found it a pain that I could not simply walk into a restaurant and get something to eat when I was hungry," he wrote. "At a number of fast food places downtown, whites could sit down and eat, but blacks could only eat standing up at the counter. I went hungry rather than subject myself to that."

He sent a letter to a local newspaper, the *Washington Star*, urging the city to desegregate its public schools. "It was the first thing I had written that I know was published."[3]

In 1960, when Sowell was in graduate school at the University of Chicago, a friend who taught at a black college in Alabama sent him some news clippings about protests in the South. Sowell wrote back that he "was very proud of the way our people have sprung to life and the good judgment with which things had been handled." He added that it was "particularly interesting that 18 of the 21 Negro restaurant workers in Atlanta refused to help the owner clear the steam table. Who would have believed this possible ten years ago?"[4]

Yet by 1962, he was already beginning to have doubts about this approach to addressing racial inequality. "The more I follow the integration struggles of the South, the more I am inclined to be skeptical as to the actual fruit of it all," he wrote in a letter to a former roommate at Harvard. "It is awkward to stand on the sidelines and criticize people who are suffering for their ideals, and yet the question must be asked, 'What is this going to *do*?' There seem to be so many other things with greater priority than equality-of-public-accommodation that the blind preoccupation with this one thing seems almost pathological." As he saw it, "the fervor generated in the fight for 'integration' in all things at all costs seems more an emotional release than a sensible movement toward something that promises a worthwhile benefit."[5]

For Sowell, it was already clear that the pursuit of equal rights involved trade-offs. Time and resources directed at one thing leaves less time and fewer resources to direct at something else. He later wrote, "Given all the urgent needs for more and better education, for example, and for all the things that can be obtained with the fruits of work skills and business experience, how much time and effort could be spared for endless campaigns to get into every hamburger stand operated by a redneck?" But in addition to thinking activists were doing a poor job of picking their battles, Sowell was increasingly bothered by the way black leaders seemed to be much too concerned with white approval. In Washington at the time, "there happened to be some fifth-rate college—I'm not even sure whether it was accredited—that would not admit blacks," he wrote. "I thought the local civil rights groups did the right thing when they denounced this racial policy, but I was appalled that they actually invested further efforts in trying to get the policy changed. Not only did this seem like an investment that ought to be put somewhere else, it annoyed me that we seemed to be constantly seeking acceptance and validation by white people—*any* white people at all, anywhere."[6]

The civil rights leadership would continue down this path in the decades to come. Well into the twenty-first century, black leaders still often seemed far more interested in seeking slavery reparations and toppling Confederate statuary than in offering poor black families an escape from failing public schools. Activists were continuing to pursue white validation as the end-all, be-all, now especially through the movement Black Lives Matter. Sowell had witnessed these trends in their earliest iterations more than a half-century ago. And it turns out that he was right to suspect that they would do little, in and of themselves, to narrow racial disparities.

THE ERA'S MAJOR CIVIL RIGHTS LEGISLATION HADN'T EVEN passed yet, but Sowell already had come around to the view that while desegregation was certainly a worthwhile goal, it was at least as important, if not more so, to ensure that blacks were undergoing the necessary self-development to advance in American society once Jim Crow was dismantled. And to his dismay, civil rights leaders increasingly were preoccupied with the former while neglecting the latter. In 1963, writing to a couple then living abroad who had been involved in sit-ins in the South, he said, "One of my ironic experiences has been hearing from a former teacher of mine who is now teaching in a Negro college in Mississippi and finding the students hopelessly backward and apathetic. Though this may seem a violation of the code of the hills or something, I am more and more frequently led to believe that much of our social reforming zeal is a colossal barking up the wrong tree."[7] The question was not whether government-mandated racial segregation should end, but whether that would be enough, by itself, to address inequalities in the long term. He made this point even more explicitly in a 1964 letter to a black graduate student:

> To me the psychology of the Negro is the biggest single obstacle to racial progress. It isn't fashionable to say this, and it certainly isn't pleasant, but truth does not depend on these considerations. With all due respect to the courage and dedication of the various civil rights groups, I think that when all the laws have been passed and all the gates flung open, the net result will be one tremendous anticlimax unless there is a drastic change of attitude among Negroes. The current pleas

for special treatment are a symptom of the attitude that needs changing and such treatment would be a big obstacle to the necessary change.[8]

In later decades, Sowell's scholarship would demonstrate empirically that racial preferences for the black underclass were not only ineffective but counterproductive, that they stigmatized black achievement, and that they were no substitute for the development of skills, attitudes, and habits that are conducive to upward mobility. But here we see inklings of what was to come. Sowell was likewise far ahead of many others in his thinking about the limited efficacy of antidiscrimination laws in addressing social inequality. In early 1964, prior to the passage later that year of landmark civil rights legislation, he wrote to a friend, "I think some individuals and groups have greatly misconceived the problem. Perhaps if the omnibus civil rights bill goes through Congress undiluted, the bitter anticlimax that is sure to follow may provoke some real thought in quarters where slogans and labels hold sway at the moment."[9]

In addition to his concern that black leaders were prioritizing racial integration to a fault, Sowell also worried that previous calls for equal treatment were now morphing into calls for special treatment. In 1963, the head of the Urban League, a civil rights organization, wrote an article in the *New York Times Magazine* calling for the preferential hiring of blacks. Sowell criticized the idea in a letter to the editor:

As a Negro, I feel that the Urban League's Whitney M. Young . . . is tragically wrong in his scheme for special treatment for Negroes—wrong not only tactically and morally, but wrong in terms of its probable effect on Negroes themselves. How can anyone seriously expect to develop initiative, respect for work and responsibility among people who are "sought" for good jobs, who receive "conscious preferment" and other semantic evasions meaning special privileges?

The difference between all the other special aids to particular groups which Mr. Young cites—G.I. Bill, etc.—and the program which he is advocating for Negroes is very simple: they were all efforts to enable a particular group to meet a certain standard, not efforts to lower the standard for them.

While Mr. Young rejects the out-and-out job quota idea, he accepts the basic reasoning behind the job quota system, that numerical underrepresentation of Negroes in certain jobs is evidence of discrimination . . .

People who have been trying for years to tell others that Negroes are basically no different from anybody else should not themselves lose sight of the fact that Negroes are just like everyone else in wanting something for nothing. The worst thing that could happen would be to hold out hopes of getting it.[10]

Sowell was neither imagining things nor overstating his case. What would turn out to be an important change in thinking was well underway in the 1960s among black elites. In the early decades of the 1900s, millions of blacks, including Sowell's own family, had migrated out of the South and settled in northern cities, where the focus was as much on self-development as it was on securing equal rights. Indeed, black self-improvement was seen as the best pathway to equal rights. As the journalist Isabel Wilkerson wrote in her book on black migration, *The Warmth of Other Suns*, black newspapers at the time, such as the *Chicago Defender*, and leading civil rights organizations, including the Urban League, "ran periodic lists of 'do's and don'ts'" that advised the new arrivals on how to behave properly: "Don't use vile language in public places." "Don't appear on the street with old dust caps, dirty aprons and ragged clothes." "Don't loaf. Get a job at once." "Do not keep your children out of school." In a 1917 editorial, the *Chicago Defender* wrote, "It is our duty . . . to guide the hand of a less experienced one, especially when one misstep weakens our chance for climbing."[11]

In the 1960s, such talk began to be regarded as passé, and in later decades it would be derided as "respectability politics." But an earlier generation of blacks that included Sowell maintained that self-regard and self-respect were essential to economic progress, and the results spoke for themselves. Census data show that in the 1940s and 1950s black poverty rates plummeted, black incomes rose at a faster rate than white incomes, and the racial gap in years of schooling narrowed from four years to less than two.[12]

SOWELL SUPPORTED THE CIVIL RIGHTS ACT OF 1964 AND the Voting Rights Act of 1965 but was remarkably prescient about their limited impact on the social and economic advancement of blacks. Many who cite these pieces of legislation as the catalysts for subsequent black progress have ignored the trends already in place before the bills were passed. In hindsight, calling these civil rights victories anticlimactic almost sounds like an understatement.

Black poverty was falling faster prior to the 1960s than it would in subsequent decades. In the 1970s and 1980s, the poorest 20 percent of blacks saw their incomes decline at more than twice the rate of comparable whites.[13] Black crime and joblessness also worsened after the 1960s. And the rates at which blacks were entering middle-class professions decreased after the implementation of affirmative action policies that were supposed to produce the exact opposite effect. As Sowell had feared, the push among blacks for *equal* treatment soon gave way to demands for quotas, set-asides, and other forms of *special* treatment.

Sowell's own writings would not explore these phenomena in depth for at least another decade, and some of his most devastating assessments of the black leadership—in *The Economics and Politics of Race, Civil Rights: Rhetoric or Reality?* and other books—would not be published until the 1980s. But the letters show how far back he had been thinking and writing critically about conventional approaches to helping blacks advance, if only in his private correspondence and the occasional letter to a newspaper. In 1970 the liberal political scientist Andrew Hacker published a lengthy defense of the Black Power movement in the *New York Times*, and Sowell responded in a letter to the editor: "I sometimes wonder if those of us who are black ought not to consider declaring some sort of moral amnesty for guilty whites, just so they won't keep on saying and doing damn fool things that create additional problems."[14]

Moreover, there is every indication that his conclusions were born of his own observations and thought processes. They didn't derive from some attempt to ingratiate himself with a particular ideology or political party, which was often the accusation, especially during the Reagan era. After

Ronald Reagan won the 1980 presidential election, and stories began to appear in the press that Sowell was being considered for secretary of the Department of Housing and Urban Development (HUD), civil rights leaders became enraged. "We would view with considerable concern the appointment of Tom Sowell to HUD or, for that matter, to any other cabinet position," said the general counsel of the NAACP. "He would play the same kind of role that historically the house niggers played for the plantation owners. He could mete out the straight discipline. No matter how inhumanely administered, it would be presumed more acceptable because the hands of the disciplinarian are black."

If such an accusation were made today, it almost certainly would be picked up by conservative talk radio, television outlets like Fox News, and right-wing social media. But none of that existed in the early 1980s, and Sowell mostly had to fend for himself. He had no interest in being HUD secretary and ultimately decided against accepting any cabinet posts. Still, there was a larger issue at stake, and Sowell decided to push back at the NAACP's smear in kind. He pointed out the hypocrisy in assuming that only blacks on the political left can take money from white benefactors and maintain their integrity. He also noted that the media's liberal bias made them blind to the growing disconnect between the priorities of civil rights groups and the priorities of the people they claimed to represent. "I think the NAACP are the classic house niggers," he told the *Washington Post*. "Their support comes from the white liberals in the press and philanthropy, and they are constantly taking positions the very opposite of the black community on crime, on quotas, on busing. What I think is tragic is that the media has bought their position."[15]

Sowell did briefly consider accepting other cabinet positions. The Department of Education had a certain appeal, because he felt better schooling would be essential to the advancement of low-income minorities. In the end, however, he decided he didn't have the temperament for politics and withdrew his name from consideration. He did agree to be a member of Reagan's Economic Policy Advisory Committee, which met a few times each year, but he resigned after the first meeting. Not only were these confabs too long for his tastes, but he was living on the West Coast at the time and had underestimated the stress of transcontinental travel.[16] He never regretted the decision to quit. In one letter, he wrote, "I am more inclined to the opinion (and the example) of Milton Friedman, that some individuals can contribute more by staying out of government."[17]

Media suggestions to the contrary notwithstanding, the reality is that Sowell was a registered Democrat until 1972 and has never been a registered Republican. "Despite media attempts to make me almost part of the Reagan administration, I remained independent of it throughout its eight years in office, and criticized it severely in print whenever I disagreed with it," he wrote in his memoir. "When my own long-standing views happened to coincide with those of the Reagan administration on a particular issue, I of course said so, but there was no attempt to be in step with them."[18] His letters give us no reason to doubt this assertion. Sowell was expressing skepticism about government efforts to help the black underclass well before Ronald Reagan was even governor of California, let alone president.

But the criticism of Sowell as a sellout is off base for another important reason. His ambitions were shaped primarily by a previous generation of *black* intellectuals—such as E. Franklin Frazier, St. Clair Drake, John Hope Franklin, Kenneth Clark, and Sterling Brown, among others—who either never got their due or received it relatively late in their careers. This was not because he would always agree with their research or conclusions on public policy, but because he so admired what these pioneers had accomplished professionally given the circumstances blacks were forced to endure in the early decades of the twentieth century. Their experiences, along with his own, helped to inform Sowell's view that black people could and should be held to the same standards as other groups. "Sowell came to intellectual maturity under the influence of this generation of black scholars," wrote the liberal black academic Jerry Watts in a lengthy profile of Sowell for *Dissent* magazine in 1982. "Few current black writers celebrate their achievements or refer to their works more often than he. What must have impressed him is their individual initiative and ultimate success in the face of far greater obstacles than blacks confront now."[19] Watts himself wrote about black intellectuals and was sharply critical of Sowell's scholarship on race, but his essay also decried attempts by other black thinkers on the left to try to dismiss Sowell as a callous race-traitor rather than addressing his arguments with counterarguments:

> Thomas Sowell is no "house nigger." That he and other blacks who attempt critically to analyze intraethnic issues are subject to this charge reflects our inability to tolerate diversity. Furthermore, in a roundabout way, it is racist, for it assumes that blacks who think "differently" are not asserting their autonomy but merely acting as an intermediary for some white interest. In

the case of Sowell, his conservatism predates his relationship with Reagan and is, in fact, more sophisticated than Reagan's . . .

As far as I can tell, he is strongly concerned with the problems of those black Americans who are not, by any definition, "making it." He certainly spends enough time writing about free-market solutions to problems confronting poor blacks. We may disagree with his prescriptions, but that he is *concerned* we cannot doubt.[20]

If Sowell's harping on the primacy of black self-development could be described as unfashionable in the 1960s, when the Urban League, the NAACP, and other groups were reassessing their own priorities and methods, it could not be described as unprecedented. If anything, Sowell's analyses are in the tradition of his fellow black forebears, not his white contemporaries. The most prominent black leaders of a previous era, including the abolitionist Frederick Douglass and the educator Booker T. Washington, shared Sowell's deep skepticism of government benevolence and the lowering of standards to facilitate black advancement. "Everybody has asked the question . . . 'What should we do with the Negro?'" said Douglass in 1865. "I have had but one answer from the beginning. Do nothing with us! Your doing with us has already played the mischief with us. Do nothing with us! If the apples will not remain on the tree of their own strength, if they are worm-eaten at the core, if they are early ripe and disposed to fall, let them fall! . . . And if the Negro cannot stand on his own legs, let him fall also. All I ask is, give him a chance to stand on his own legs!"[21]

Washington, who, like Douglass, was born a slave, said, in his famous Atlanta Exposition speech, "It is important and right that all privileges of the law be ours, but it is vastly more important that we be prepared for the exercise of these privileges."[22]

The black sociologist W. E. B. Du Bois had his differences with Washington over whether civil rights or self-improvement should be the principal goal of blacks in the first decades of the twentieth century, but both men agreed that white racism was hardly the only, or even the biggest, obstacle that blacks would face during Jim Crow or in its aftermath. In his 1895 book, *The Souls of Black Folk*, Du Bois lamented, referring to young blacks, especially, for whom slavery was at best a "dim recollection," that the world "asked little of them, and they answered with little." Many had "[sunk] into listless indifference, or shiftlessness, or reckless bravado."[23] He later wrote that even if whites were suddenly to abandon their racial prejudices, the immediate impact on the economic conditions of most blacks would be minimal. Sounding very much like a future Thomas Sowell, Du Bois said that "some few would be promoted," but "the mass would remain as they are," until the younger generation began to "try harder" and the entire race "lost the omnipresent excuse for failure: prejudice."[24] Douglass, Washington, and Du Bois would not live to see the passage of legislation in the 1960s that finally extended equal rights to blacks, but they were optimistic that such a day would come. Like Sowell, they believed that when it did, it was of paramount importance that blacks be equipped with the habits and attitudes and skills necessary to take full advantage of what America had to offer.

3

HIGHER EDUCATION, LOWER EXPECTATIONS

"The double standard of grades and
degrees is an open secret on many
campuses, and it is only a matter of
time before it is an open secret among
employers as well."

THE FIRST DECADE OF SOWELL'S ACADEMIC CAREER WAS THE
1960s, and he spent it mostly teaching, completing work
on his PhD, and writing about economic theory. But the
1960s were also years of tremendous social unrest in
America, marked by mass protests against racism, sexism,
and the war in Vietnam as well as by rapidly evolving mo-
res. Much of this turmoil played out on college campuses,
where Sowell, then in his thirties, was trying to settle into
the life of a professor. His preference was classroom teaching, as opposed to research, but his methods and sensibili-
ties were on a collision course with the spirit of the times.
By the late 1960s he was already having second thoughts
about a career in academia. "The small college has always
had a certain appeal to me, but the big question mark has
always been whether the closer student-faculty relationship

which is possible there is utilized for intellectual purposes" or for "artificially extending the students' adolescence," he wrote to a friend in 1968. "The idea of emphasizing teaching appeals to me, but too often 'teaching' means student public relations, and is judged by how happy you keep them rather than how much they learn."[1]

These reservations developed during a period when Sowell had been thriving as a scholar. His first academic article, on Karl Marx's prediction of "increasing misery" for workers under capitalism, was published in 1960 in the *American Economic Review*, widely considered the top journal in the field. His first book, an introductory textbook for undergraduate college students titled *Economics: Analysis and Issues*, would come in 1971. In between, he wrote about Thorstein Veblen, Thomas Malthus, David Ricardo, and other influential economists for scholarly journals, including *Oxford Economic Papers*, *Economica*, and the *Canadian Journal of Economics and Political Science*. At the time, there was greater interest in Sowell's specialty, the history of economic thought, in England and Canada than in the United States, so most of his professional writing during this period was published in foreign journals. "Though I did not realize it at the time, this was a long-term blessing," he wrote many years later. "The economists who ran these journals in other countries had no way of knowing what color I was, so I was spared the doubts that became increasingly common over the years among black academics, as to whether their achievements were really their own or were due to tokenism or double standards applied by whites."[2]

Although he is best known today for his views on culture and ethnicity, Sowell didn't set out in that direction and would write extensively on many nonracial issues over the decades. He would publish books on such diverse topics as late-talking children, choosing a college, and the housing boom that led to the 2008 subprime mortgage crisis. Without counting the ten bound collections of his writings and updated editions of earlier works, he produced thirty-six books between 1971 and 2018. The first one didn't appear until he was already forty years old, most are still in print, and nearly two-thirds of them center on topics other than race. His best-selling title is *Basic Economics: A Common Sense Guide to the Economy*, which has been translated into six other languages, and he's proudest of his books on social theory and the history of ideas.

When Sowell did eventually start weighing in publicly on racial controversies, it was out of frustration at the general direction of the public discussion, not because he craved notoriety. Nor was he compelled to do so because he couldn't make a living by working on other matters; he'd done precisely that in the 1960s. Rather, he saw his commentary on these issues as an act of public service, or even a duty. "One of the melancholy features of being over forty is that many things which seem new, unprecedented, and exciting to the young begin to look like tired reruns of an old movie on the late, late show," he wrote in *Black Education: Myths and Tragedies*, a book that reflects on his teaching career. "As one who specializes in the history of economic and social thought, I may be more prone to this reaction than some others. It is depressing to hear ideas trumpeted as *New!* when the underlying reasoning involved was common in the 1840s or the 1790s—and discredited by the 1920s." And he was especially suspect of activists pushing agendas that didn't necessarily comport with the needs or desires of the people they claimed to represent, writing, for example, "The black community has long been plagued by spellbinding orators who know how to turn the hopes and fears of others into dollars and cents for themselves." Here, Sowell was speaking not only as a scholar but also from personal experience. "The current militant rhetoric, self-righteousness and lifestyle are painfully old to me," he continued. "I have seen the same intonations, the same cadence, the same crowd manipulation techniques, the same visions of mystical redemption, the same faith that certain costumes, gestures, phrases and group emotional release would somehow lead to the Promised Land. And I have seen the same hustling messiahs driving their Cadillacs and getting their pictures in the paper."[3]

SOWELL HAD BEEN CURIOUS FROM A YOUNG AGE ABOUT THE causes of inequality. It's what motivated him to study economics and history in the first place. Initially, this pursuit was for his own personal benefit, an attempt to comprehend the world around him. From there, he set about sharing what he'd learned. The goal was not to berate or belittle others but to leave people better informed—particularly those in a position to make important decisions for themselves or for society. As he once put it, "Most of my writings on public policy issues in general, and on racial issues in particular, were directed toward the public or toward policy-makers and tried to show where one policy would be better than another."[4]

What distinguished Sowell to some extent was not so much what he believed but what he had the gumption to express publicly. Even other scholars who sympathized with his point of view about the so-called "Negro prob-lem" were reluctant to say so for fear of being personally vilified and having it damage their careers. After Daniel Patrick Moynihan, then President Lyndon B. Johnson's assistant secretary of labor, noted, in a 1965 government study of the black family, that the growing number of black children born to single mothers was bound to hin-der the future social and economic progress of blacks, civil rights leaders, politicians, commentators, and other critics denounced Moynihan as a bigot who was "blaming the victim."[5] And when two well-regarded social scientists, Christopher Jencks and David Riesman, published a frank and comprehensive critique of black colleges in a 1967 is-sue of the *Harvard Educational Review*, they received sim-ilar treatment.[6]

But popularity wasn't a paramount concern of Sow-ell's, who knew he had a thick skin when it came to crit-icism and wasn't easily intimidated. He felt a personal obligation to weigh in with an alternative perspective on racial topics. He believed that the basic assumptions be-hind many of the policies aimed at minorities needed to be better scrutinized and felt that too few public intellec-tuals were interested in speaking out. "I had been subject to criticism for all kinds of other things long before I got into racial issues," he explained. "I can remember one of my roommates in college saying that something I did at Harvard really had rubbed people the wrong way. I said, 'You can't please all the people, all the time.' And he said, 'You're not pleasing any of the people, any of the time.'"[7] Sowell also felt he was acting in the tradition of black in-tellectual forebears who followed the facts even when they led to unpopular conclusions. "E. Franklin Frazier caught this [flak] too," he said, in reference to a distinguished black sociologist who had taught at Howard University in the 1950s. Frazier had painted a devastating picture of black elites in his 1957 book, *Black Bourgeoisie*. "He was an empiricist. He was from the Chicago school of sociology," said Sowell. "He did not pull any punches. I'm told that there were places at Howard University where there would be a committee meeting, and when Frazier walked into a room, people would get up and walk out."[8]

Black Bourgeoisie first appeared in France in 1955, and in the preface to the US edition, released two years later, Frazier responded to the negative reaction among some American blacks. "They did not challenge the truth of the picture that had been presented so much as they were shocked that a Negro would dare place on display their behavior and innermost thoughts," he wrote. "Following the initial shock of self-revelation was intense anger on the part of many leaders in the Negro community. This anger was based largely upon their feeling that I had betrayed Negroes by revealing their life to the white world. I was attacked by some Negroes as being bitter . . . and by others as having been paid to defame the Negro."[9]

Of course, the very same criticisms would be directed at Sowell throughout his career as a public intellectual. He was well aware that such attacks were nothing new, and, like Frazier, he believed they were worth enduring— that any scholar with any integrity had no other choice. Black intellectuals preoccupied with "protecting the image of blacks in the eyes of whites" were missing the boat, as Sowell saw things. Better to focus on "knowing what the facts were, as a basis for whatever was to be done to make things better."[10]

Time and again throughout his career, Sowell was willing to take personal and professional risks to adhere to his principles. He took it upon himself to challenge orthodoxies, reject circumspection, and say straightforwardly what others would not. "It has not been a pleasure to write this book but a necessity," he said in the introduction to *Civil Rights: Rhetoric or Reality?*, his 1984 book about the civil rights movement. And in the preface to *Black Rednecks and White Liberals*, a 2005 tome on the historical development of ghetto culture, he wrote, "Many of the facts cited here may be surprising or even startling to some readers, but they are not literally unknown to scholars; they have simply not been widely discussed in the media or even in academia." His job was to pursue the truth, and sugarcoating it, he thought, was no way to help black people advance. "Unfortunately, there are very few people who take positions similar to mine," he told C-SPAN interviewer Brian Lamb in 1990. "And if that viewpoint is to be heard at all, I'm going to have to be the one that does a lot of [the talking]."[11]

Sowell has stressed that he began writing about racial controversies primarily "because there is something that needs to be said—and because other people have better sense than to say it."[12] He stayed the course even though colleagues suggested to him that, as he put it, "I would be better off to stop writing about race and to return to the things in which I did my best professional work—books on economics like *Knowledge and Decisions* or books on ideas like *A Conflict of Visions* and *The Quest for Cosmic Justice*."[13] His decision to ignore that advice and continue questioning conventional explanations for racial inequality is one of his most important legacies, and his extensive writings on race and culture will be discussed in greater detail in the chapters that follow. What's important to note here is the extent to which the racial controversies of the 1960s and 1970s, in academia in particular, served to thwart Sowell's teaching ambitions while also influencing key aspects of his scholarship for the rest of his career.

AFFIRMATIVE ACTION IN COLLEGE ADMISSIONS BEGAN IN the 1960s, and the focus initially was on locating minority candidates for better jobs and educational opportunities. But by the end of the decade that focus had shifted, particularly at elite schools, where less qualified minority students were being admitted under de facto racial quotas. By the early 1970s, "affirmative action came to mean much more than advertising opportunities actively, seeking out those who might not know of them, and preparing those who might not yet be qualified," wrote the sociologist Nathan Glazer. "It came to mean the setting of statistical requirements based on race, color, and national origin for employers and educational institutions."[14] One result was increased ambivalence about the merits of black achievement, not only among whites but also among the intended beneficiaries. Derrick Bell, a black law professor, denounced the "benevolent paternalism" of a racial double standard for blacks in a 1970 law review article. It results, he wrote, in "feelings of inferiority in the students' hearts and minds in a way unlikely ever to be undone." Moreover, he added, "it robs those black students who have done well from receiving real credit and the boost in confidence that their accomplishments merit."[15] Race-based admissions also led to a demand for black studies departments, and out of expediency many schools eagerly acquiesced. "It was far easier for universities to establish Afro-American studies departments than to place blacks in traditional academic disciplines," wrote Jerry Watts, a black academic who attended Harvard in the 1970s. "Nor was this the only tragedy. Black studies departments in numerous instances facilitated the hiring of black faculty who would not have qualified for the job had their scholarly work been the primary criteria." According to Watts, Sowell was one of the few people at the time who were "willing to discuss this aspect of the black studies phenomenon. Whites feared being called racist and black faculty stood to benefit."[16]

In his memoir, *My Grandfather's Son*, Supreme Court Justice Clarence Thomas related his frustration while job-hunting in his final year at Yale Law School, where he graduated in 1974. "One high-priced lawyer after another treated me dismissively, making it clear that they had no interest in me despite my Ivy League pedigree," he wrote. "Many asked pointed questions unsubtly suggesting that they doubted I was as smart as my grades indicated." Thomas eventually stopped interviewing with big-city firms altogether and took a job with the state attorney general's office in Missouri. "Now I knew what a law degree from Yale was worth when it bore the taint of racial preference," he wrote.[17] In a 1970 essay, Sowell had anticipated Thomas's ordeal. "The double standard of grades and degrees is an open secret on many campuses, and it is only a matter of time before it is an open secret among employers as well," he predicted. "The market can be ruthless in devaluing degrees that do not mean what they say. It should be apparent to anyone not blinded by his own nobility that it also devalues the student in his own eyes."[18]

Of course, some blacks minimized the downstream effect of racial preferences. Randall Kennedy, a black professor at Harvard Law School, has said publicly that he was offered a teaching post there despite not meeting the school's usual standards. He suspects that Harvard "took extra steps to recruit me because they wanted to add some color" to the faculty in the mid-1980s. According to Kennedy, affirmative action also played a role in his being admitted to prestigious academic societies like the American Academy of Arts and Sciences. Still, he wrote that he did not "feel belittled by this": "Nor am I wracked by angst or guilt or self-doubt," even though some "will put a mental asterisk next to my name upon learning that my race (almost certainly) counted as a plus in the process of selecting me."[19] Like other supporters of affirmative action, Kennedy argues that these practices help to rectify past wrongs committed against blacks, which is more important to him than any cloud of suspicion they create around black accomplishments.

But John McWhorter, a black professor of humanities at Columbia University, has countered that we shouldn't be so quick to dismiss the psychological toll of racial double standards. "The white student who gets a letter announcing his admission to Duke can go out and celebrate a signal achievement, although the luck of the draw almost always plays some role in a white or Asian person's admission to a school," he wrote. "Can the black middle-manager's daughter getting the same letter have the same sense of achievement if her SAT scores and grades would have barred any white or Asian from admission? The truth is no—she can only celebrate having been good enough *among African-American students* to be admitted."[20]

One of the more thoughtful meditations on racial preferences and stigma is Yale law professor Stephen Carter's *Reflections of an Affirmative Action Baby*. In the 1970s, Carter attended Stanford University as an undergraduate and then applied to Harvard Law School. He was initially rejected but then received phone calls from school officials who wanted to apologize for the mix-up:

> They were quite frank in their explanation of the "error." I was told by one official that the school had initially rejected me because "we assumed from your record that you were white." (The words have always stuck in my mind, a tantalizing reminder of what is expected of me.) Suddenly coy, he went on to say that the school had obtained "additional information that should have been counted in your favor"—that is, Harvard had discovered the color of my skin . . .
>
> Naturally, I was insulted . . . Stephen Carter, the white male, was not good enough for Harvard Law School; Stephen Carter, the black male, not only was good enough but rated agonized telephone calls urging him to attend. And Stephen Carter, color unknown, must have been white: How else could he have achieved what he did in college?[21]

Sowell credits dumb luck with saving him from all this personal second-guessing. His accomplishments happened to predate policies that lowered standards for blacks. The timing was "fortuitous," he wrote. "My academic career began two years before the Civil Rights Act of 1964 and

I received tenure a year before federal 'goals and timetables' were mandated under affirmative action policies." This timing "spared me the hang-ups afflicting many other black intellectuals, who were haunted by the idea that they owed their careers to affirmative action or to the fact that writings on race had become fashionable."[22]

Yet the timing worked against Sowell in other respects. He wanted to be a college professor more than anything, but the atmosphere on campuses was changing in the 1960s, and in ways that he could not or would not abide. One of the most astute observers of this evolution was Allan Bloom, the political philosopher and classicist who taught at Cornell in the late 1960s, when Sowell was also on the faculty there. Bloom published a scathing essay in 1969 lamenting what he described as the increasing "democratization" of the university, which he attributed primarily to the student protest movement: "Each student is to be permitted to construct his own curriculum and discover his special genius or realize his unique self," he wrote, and the university "can no longer provide guidance as to what is important and set standards." In this new way of thinking about college, the "whole of education must be guided by the standard of relevance" as determined by the most outspoken and ideological students on campus. "Those students who are doing most of the talking and popularizing the notion of relevance—that is, the Leftist students—mean that education must be directed to the problems of war, poverty, and, particularly, racism as they now present themselves."[23]

Nearly two decades later, in his 1987 best seller, *The Closing of the American Mind*, Bloom would expand on his critique of how the academy had lost its way and become captive to a type of thinking that higher education previously had sought to dispel. He wrote that in the 1960s, the universities "gave way under the pressure of mass movements and did so in large measure because they thought those movements possessed a moral truth superior to any the university could provide. Commitment was understood to be profounder than science, passion than reason, history than nature, the young than the old."[24] The "New Left" in America was presenting an "unthinking hatred of 'bourgeois society,'" and too few of the faculty and administrators on campus were willing and able to push back with a coherent explanation of the proper role of a university. As a result, students "discerned that their teachers did not really believe that freedom of thought was necessarily a good and useful thing, that they suspected all this was ideology protecting the injustices of our 'system,' and that they could be pressured into benevolence toward violent attempts to change the ideology."[25] Bloom went on to describe a mindset of the period that warrants being quoted at some length. Sowell had embarked on a teaching career in an academic world that was increasingly unrecognizable from the one he himself had inhabited as a student. He had every intention of holding students to the same standards to which he had been held, but Bloom explained why that had become so controversial:

> About the sixties it is now fashionable to say that although there were indeed excesses, many good things resulted. But, so far as universities are concerned, I know of nothing positive coming from that period; it was an unmitigated disaster for them. I hear that the good things were "greater openness," "less rigidity,"

"freedom from authority," etc.—but these have no content and express no view of what is wanted from a university education. During the sixties I sat on various committees at Cornell and continuously and futilely voted against dropping one requirement after the next. The old core curriculum—according to which every student in the college had to take a smattering of courses in the major divisions of knowledge—was abandoned. One professor of comparative literature . . . explained that these requirements taught little, really did not introduce students to the various disciplines, and bored them. I admitted this to be true. He then expressed surprise at my unwillingness to give them up. It was because they were, I said, a threadbare reminiscence of the unity of knowledge and provided an obstinate little hint that there are some things one must know about if one is to be educated. You don't replace something with nothing. Of course, that was exactly what the educational reform of the sixties was doing.[26]

Sowell's very first academic post was at Douglass College, a women's college at Rutgers University in New Jersey, where he was hired in 1962 to teach economics. He liked the small-campus feel and had positive interactions with the students—"I decided that this is how I wanted to spend my life"—but the sentiment was fleeting.[27] Due to constant run-ins with colleagues over his teaching style and tough grading, he tendered his resignation after only a year—a pattern that would repeat itself at other schools. After accepting a post at Howard University in 1963, he became dismayed by, among other things, the lax standards and seeming indifference among administrators to the "blatant, organized and pervasive" cheating on exams.[28] "The common run of students at Howard are almost unbelievably lazy, dishonest, rude and irresponsible," he wrote to a friend at the time. But even more troubling was the school's indulgence of this behavior. "All too frequently the school panders to their worst habits by giving deadline extensions, make-up exams, Incompletes . . . etc. to the point where these things are regarded almost as Constitutional rights."[29]

The experience at Howard hit him especially hard. Sowell had attended the school as an undergraduate before transferring to Harvard and understood the unique challenges that black colleges faced. In graduate school at Columbia, he and another black student had spent hours discussing all manner of ways to improve black colleges, and he had every intention of joining the faculty at such a school one day. He made inquiries about teaching at several black schools, including the Tuskegee Institute in Alabama and Morgan State College in Maryland, before settling on Howard. And he took the job there even though better schools had expressed an interest in hiring him. His mentor Milton Friedman recalled the decision:

> He talked to several of us about which [offer] to accept, expressing a strong preference for accepting one of the least attractive offers—at Howard University in Washington—on the purely emotional ground that it would enable him to make the greatest contribution to the improvement of members of his race. I tried to dissuade him—as did others of my colleagues. I urged on him that he would do far more for blacks by

demonstrating that he could compete successfully in the largely white scholarly world as a whole than by teaching at a predominantly black institution which was less renowned in scholarship and research than other institutions from which he had offers. Despite all the advice, Tom insisted on going to Howard.[30]

It was hardly the first time that Sowell had opted to experience something for himself rather than taking someone's word for it, and it wouldn't be the last. But it also illustrated his deep belief that education plays an essential role in black advancement. Education had lifted him out of poverty and into the middle class, and he had no doubt that it could do the same for others, regardless of whatever else blacks in the United States had stacked against them. Today, fewer than 10 percent of black college students attend black colleges.[31] But in the early 1960s these schools played a central role in black higher education—particularly in the South, where most blacks lived. In 1965, an estimated three-quarters of all black college students in the South attended black colleges, and by 1970 it was still well over half.[32] Sowell wanted to go where the black students were, where the problem was most pronounced, and where he thought he was most needed. "I knew that . . . behind many of these kids was some father driving a cab at night, after working all day, or some mother down on her knees scrubbing some white woman's floor, in order to send their children to college to try and make something out of them."[33]

He wanted to help improve the situation at black colleges but didn't fully appreciate the forces he'd be up against. These included not only overcoming the substandard elementary and high school education that blacks had received, but also dealing with the "maudlin sort of liberal, frequently a white instructor," who asked so little of black students once they got to college. "From these and others one hears a lot of give-the-poor-kids-a-break arguments and you-can't-expect-too-much warnings," Sowell wrote to a friend who taught at another college. He challenged his students and rejected the idea that you help blacks progress by holding them to lower standards. "Actually, these kids are infinitely further advanced in the ability department than they are in the attitude department," he told his friend. "Whenever you can get them to do the reading . . . they usually show themselves quite capable of handling it. But why should they do the work, when the university makes it so much easier for them to alibi, cheat, whine or intrigue?"[34] Fed up with the "anti-intellectual" and "corrupt" environment at the school, he left after only a year.

Wiser to the ways of the academy, Sowell sought and received assurances that there would be no interference with his teaching before he accepted his next academic post. Cornell University hired him in 1965, and he taught there until 1969 while completing work on his doctorate. It was the Cornell experience, perhaps more than any other in academia before or after, that crystallized his view that higher education was on a perilous course. By the late 1960s, student disruptions on campus had become commonplace, and Sowell was disappointed by the inept and cowardly response of university administrators unwilling to stand their ground. He refused to cancel classes to accommodate student demonstrations. Nor would he allow class discussions to veer off toward current events unrelated to the course. "Academia changed," he told me. "I did not grade on the curve and I did not give a passing grade to someone who knew nothing more, functionally, than when he came to the class. And that usually made me a standout wherever I was."*

It wasn't the only thing that made him a standout. Sowell was also becoming a first-rate scholar. While teaching at Douglass, where he was the first black male instructor the school had ever hired, several prestigious academic publications accepted his article submissions. Some of his colleagues at the school, he later noted, "would never appear in even one journal of the same caliber in their whole careers."[35] After Sowell accepted Cornell's offer, he discovered that he was the only black faculty member on campus. But if "there were any suspicions that I was a 'token' black appointment, such suspicions were probably minimized by the fact that I had published more than any of the other assistant professors of economics, and perhaps more than all of them put together."[36] During his teaching career, Sowell would field offers from other Ivy League schools as well as from top-tier state universities and liberal arts colleges. There aren't very many academics who can say they spurned offers from Stanford, Dartmouth, and the University of Wisconsin, and Sowell is among them. Had he wanted to, he almost certainly could have spent his entire career at any number of the country's most prestigious colleges and universities, secure in the knowledge that he had been hired based on his ability and not

---

* One exception, Sowell noted, was UCLA, where he taught in the 1970s and which had a reputation as a bastion of "Chicago school" economists. "At UCLA, the department flunked a fourth of the class," Sowell said. "We were second only to chemistry." Interview with author, December 29, 2015.

his skin color. "I happened to come along right after the worst of the discrimination was no longer there to impede me and just before racial quotas made the achievements of blacks look suspect."[37]

Yet by the time Sowell finally received his PhD, in December 1968, he was already having second thoughts about remaining in academia. In early 1969, he told a friend the degree had "become virtually worthless, with the academic scene being what it is. There are plenty of job offers, but almost all of them would put me right in the middle of confrontations in a period when rationality has gone out the window." By the late 1960s, black professors were expected to be not just mentors to black students, but also something akin to racial "gurus" who actively partook in campus politics. However, it was more than student militancy and spineless administrators that frustrated Sowell. The humanities and social sciences were also under assault. Curricula were being reworked to accommodate ideological fashions. Race and gender and class were becoming preoccupations in student scholarship and faculty tenure decisions. And the notion that education must be "relevant" to the students—especially to minority students from different backgrounds—was ascendant.

Shelby Steele, a scholar at the Hoover Institution who has specialized in the study of race relations, wrote that the 1960s "was arguably the most fundamentally transformative decade in American history."[38] It was the decade in which the civil rights movement, the women's movement, and the antiwar movement all gained legitimacy, thanks in no small part to the academy's willingness to serve as a platform and conduit. "By 1968 you could question virtually anything," according to Steele. "You could question your religion; the 'relevance' of a college education; the value of monogamy in marriage; the draconian laws against drug use; a college curriculum grounded solely in Western civilization; the military draft; capitalism; the taboos against interracial marriage and homosexuality; the view of pregnancy as an absolute commandment to give birth," and myriad other conventions. "The 1960s made disassociation from traditional America the very essence of a new American obsession: 'authenticity.'"[39]

THE ISSUE HERE ISN'T WHETHER THOSE CHANGES WERE good or bad or something in between. The point is that they were dramatic and happening simultaneously over a relatively short period of time. American conventions had come under siege, and higher education in the main was adrift, both in terms of what was now expected of professors and students and in terms of how schools were diversifying campuses. Sowell had first seen signs of this at Douglass College years earlier. When he arrived there in the fall of 1962, he and two other instructors assigned to teach the introductory economics course met to discuss the reading material. Two of the books for the course— Paul Samuelson's *Economics* and Robert Heilbroner's *The Worldly Philosophers*—had been chosen the previous spring before he was hired, and Sowell was asked what he thought of them. "I said the Samuelson book is fine. I learned economics from that myself. And then they asked me about Heilbroner and I expressed some reservations. They pressed me, and finally I said, 'You know, it's not worth the paper it's printed on.'" After Sowell detailed some of his problems with the book, including factual errors and what he characterized as Heilbroner's fundamentally misguided approach to economic analysis in general, his colleagues responded not by offering a defense of the text but by noting the book's popularity.

"But the students like it," they responded.[40]

That refrain—*the students like it*—"was to become a familiar one in justification of many questionable education practices" at Douglass and elsewhere, Sowell recalled.[41] Yet he was by no means persuaded that colleges should be in the business of allowing students so much latitude in determining what was and was not relevant to their learning. For starters, his own personal experiences urged caution. In Milton Friedman's price theory course at the University of Chicago, Sowell had been assigned to read a particular essay by Friedrich Hayek that he would not fully appreciate until nearly two decades later, when it inspired him to write *Knowledge and Decisions*, a book that would change his career path.

And there were other examples. As an undergraduate majoring in economics at Harvard, Sowell had been required to take French, a course that he disliked intensely, seeing no use for it at the time in his pursuit of a degree in economics. But years later, the language would prove essential to his dissertation on the theories of French classical economist Jean-Baptiste Say, who developed the doctrine that became known as Say's Law. It turned out that the writings of one of Say's contemporaries, the nineteenth-century Swiss economist Jean-Charles-Léonard Simonde de Sismondi, were quite relevant to Sowell's own interpretation of Say. Sismondi wrote mostly in French. "And so I ended up having to read a half-dozen books in French, including the fifth edition of Say's *Treatise*, where he begins to take into account what Sismondi has said and to make fundamental adjustments to Say's Law," said Sowell. "And to this day, I don't know of anybody else who has the same interpretation [that I do] because I don't know of anybody else who has bothered to read the fifth edition. The fourth edition was translated into English, but not the fifth."[42]

Sowell was pursuing a master's degree at Columbia in 1958 when he first encountered Gary Becker, the future Nobel Prize–winning economist. He signed up for Becker's yearlong labor economics course but found himself bored in class. At the end of the first semester, he approached the department chairman to ask for permission to drop the course because he didn't think he was learning anything. Permission was granted, and it would be decades later before Sowell realized his mistake. In an emotional column written after Becker died in 2014, Sowell said that his former professor had been "introducing his own analytical framework that was destined to change the way many issues would be seen by the economics profession in the years ahead." Becker was teaching "something important, but I just wasn't on the same wavelength." Sowell described his youthful arrogance as "a continuing source of embarrassment to me over the years, after I belatedly grasped what he was trying to get across." His takeaway from these episodes and others was that students often don't know—because they *can't* know at the time—what is "relevant" to their education.[43] "Lots of decisions I made, of which the change from Marxism was just one, led me to be enormously skeptical of the idea of students having a voice in creating their own courses and so forth," he said. "What you need to know to make such a decision is what you will learn years later. When you're there you don't know what the hell you're talking about."[44]

Sowell was a colleague of Allan Bloom's at Cornell in the late 1960s and largely shared Bloom's assessment of what was happening to higher education. In 1966, three years before Bloom published his essay about the ongoing democratization of the university, Sowell had written about problems with the "'democratic' approach to college education" and the drawbacks of "flinging the college gates open to all who knock." The goal of higher education, in Sowell's view, was not to maximize college attendance rates at any cost, but to attract those students who were most likely to gain something meaningful from the experience. Expanding the socioeconomic pool from which schools chose students was the right thing to do, especially given the way these institutions had discriminated against certain groups in the past. Still, college administrators shouldn't "thoughtlessly sentimentalize mass education," which could only result in the deterioration of academic standards at the expense of the more capable students who were there to learn. Sowell complained that schools increasingly were wasting time and money on students "who [didn't] care," while treating those who did care like liabilities. He illustrated this trend with an anecdote:

> A department chairman in a well-known state university once urged me to aim my teaching at the poorer students and suggested keeping the better students 'busy' with additional assignments and the like. In other words, the students who really came to get an education and who were capable of doing

so were to be treated as a problem; we were not organized to handle queer ducks like these. The chairman's attitude was by no means rare. Sometimes
it's called being "practical" or simply dealing with
the students "as they are." It could equally be called
Gresham's Law.[45]

Sowell would pick up on this theme a few years later
in a short 1969 essay on the rapid proliferation of black
studies departments at colleges and universities, particularly at the more selective schools that were most eager to
diversify their student bodies. He didn't necessarily have a
problem with schools recruiting more black students, or
even with adapting their curricula to include specialized
studies of minority groups who had long been neglected.
What troubled him was how colleges had gone about pursuing those objectives. In theory, there was nothing wrong
with creating a department devoted to history, sociology,
literature, art, and so on from a black perspective. But pro-
ponents also needed to recognize the constraints in place at
the time, including the dearth of academics with the expertise to set up programs that would be sufficiently rigorous.

"A handful of colleges and universities could establish
good programs or departments in black studies with the
scholars and material currently available," he wrote. "But
when hundreds of them try to do so simultaneously, the
existing resources are spread so thin that the result must
be something that amounts to a fraud and a criminal waste
of time for students whose intellectual skills will be desperately needed by the black community."[46] Sowell's growing
suspicion was that colleges and universities weren't really
serious about educating blacks. Rather, they wanted more

blacks matriculating on campus for the sake of appearances, and they were setting up black studies departments haphazardly as a "pay-off to prevent campus disruption."[47]

It was more evidence of how easily idealistic attempts to indulge students by making college education more "relevant" could turn counterproductive in practice. "Actually, some of the most relevant studies for dealing with ghetto needs would be medicine, law and business administration," he wrote. "Black people must be able to provide for themselves, cure themselves and defend themselves against injustices, under integration, separation, or whatever." Instead, too many of these programs were steering black students into faux "disciplines" where they didn't have to meet the same academic requirements as their nonblack peers. He feared that black studies would become "merely a euphemism for black political centers housed on college grounds," with shoddy standards for faculty and students alike. "Like many other things, black studies can be good as a principle and disastrous as a fetish," he warned. "It cannot take the place of fundamental intellectual skills, or excuse a copping-out from competition with white students. . . . There are many ways of serving black people, abandoning black people, and exploiting the suffering of black people. Black studies can play any of these roles."[48]

SOWELL'S CONCERNS CAME TO A HEAD AT CORNELL UNIversity. For a short time after leaving Howard University, before coming to Cornell, he worked as an economist for AT&T in New York. The private sector paid better than academia but left little time for completing his doctoral dissertation, so he reluctantly decided to return to teaching. He hadn't missed the academic environment at Howard, but he did miss some of his former students, and he felt conflicted about having walked out on them after only a year.

The problem was not that black schools couldn't attract good teachers, but that they couldn't hold on to them. During his two semesters teaching at Howard, Sowell said he "witnessed the departure of economists who went to teach at three Ivy League universities, to work for corporations that are household words, and one who set up his own consulting firm. There is little doubt that each of these men would have been willing to spend their lives building up that department if they thought there was any real hope of doing so."[49] Ultimately, he followed them out the door, having likewise determined that the institutional forces protecting the status quo were too powerful for him to overcome. When word of his resignation spread around Howard, "a number of students came to me to express their appreciation for what I had done, many confessing that they had misjudged me, and a couple getting angry that I was 'copping out,'" he later wrote. "One student said, 'How are we ever going to advance if people like you come here for a year and just leave?'" but Sowell had no answer for him.[50]

Of course, this was a period of social upheaval off-campus as well. And by the mid-1960s, Sowell felt a "sense of being on the sidelines on the racial developments of the times."[51] That's why one of the first things he did upon arriving at Cornell was to contact his former Howard students and gauge their interest in working at AT&T, where he still had connections. It's also why he leapt at the opportunity to help Cornell reach out to more black students.

Black undergraduates were a rarity on campus when he started teaching at the school, but their numbers were growing, and the administration had made it known that increasing minority student enrollment was a top priority.

The problem, Sowell later learned, was that Cornell had been admitting black students who did not meet its normal academic standards. In many cases, these were kids who scored above the national average on standardized tests but well below the average of other students at Cornell. The result was that by the late 1960s, half of the school's black students were on academic probation.[52] Smart black kids, who through no fault of their own were underprepared for the pace and complexity of the teaching at an elite school, and who in all likelihood would have been thriving at a less selective institution, were instead struggling at Cornell. Put another way, black students who would have been excelling at most of the nation's colleges—and thus graduating and joining middle-class professions—were being turned into failures at Cornell, all in the name of "diversity." And the problem wasn't unique to Cornell.

Moreover, qualified black students were being turned away from some outreach programs that prioritized "high-risk" minorities. Harvard, for example, had a summer program for black students interested in medical school, but the program rejected the most promising applicants as overqualified. Sowell learned of a black student who applied to the Harvard program and received a form letter in response that said, "It is the feeling of the Admissions Committee that your current qualifications are outstanding and should be strong enough to make you a viable candidate for admission to medical or dental school, without the help of this program."[53] An irritated Sowell later contacted one of the program administrators. "What sort of grotesque situation have we talked ourselves into when promising pre-med students are passed over in favor of 'high risk' students?" he wrote to the official. "The term 'high risk' has particularly grim overtones in a field where today's student will tomorrow have lives in his hands. Would you want your children to be operated on by the people you are accepting or the people you are rejecting for having outstanding qualifications?"[54]

Sowell saw such policies as unwittingly setting the stage for the campus disruptions that soon followed. "Failing and frustrated black students were ripe for demagogues blaming all their troubles on 'racism' and urging militant action," he wrote.[55] Cornell had focused on recruiting black students "by socio-political criteria, disdaining 'conventional' or 'academic' credentials or standards."[56] Even worse, as with the Harvard program, "some academically able black applicants for admission were known to have been turned away, while those who fit the stereotype being sought were admitted with lower qualifications."[57] A related problem was that the school neglected to consider the precarious financial situation of many black students. Financial aid policies "were geared more toward maximizing the body count of black students than toward adequately financing each student," which meant that "students with very serious academic deficiencies were forced to work at part-time jobs instead of spending their time making up for the education they had not received in the public schools."[58]

SOWELL SAW AN OPPORTUNITY TO HELP CHANGE THIS dynamic when the Rockefeller Foundation approached him in 1968 about setting up a summer program to bring students from black colleges to Cornell to train in economics. The university was looking for potential graduate-school candidates, and he was eager to help vet prospects. Sowell immediately agreed to head the project. He worked the phones, traveled to black colleges in search of recruits, and placed ads in campus newspapers. "Going through my grapevine, I was able to reach a number of good people on a number of black college campuses," he wrote of the experience. "The response was tremendous, both quantitatively and qualitatively. On a campus where officials said that I would not be able to find students who could qualify, I found not only students who would qualify but even some students with test scores comparable to those in the Ivy League."[59] Cornell, like other schools, had argued that it had no choice but to lower standards and focus on "high-risk" prospects to diversify the campus because there weren't enough black students who otherwise would qualify for admission. But Sowell's recruitment efforts for his summer program had clearly undermined such claims.

When Sowell arrived at Cornell, he was told that there would be no interference with his teaching. Alas, those assurances turned out to be false. During his first semester, he taught an introductory economics course for engineering students, who apparently thought they would be able to coast through class. He taught in part through class discussion, and students were expected to show up prepared to participate. Many of the engineering students did not, and a large number of them failed the first exam. On one occasion, a student was absent on the day of a test, without authorization, and Sowell refused to excuse it. In both instances, student complaints reached the department chairman and other school officials, who then leaned on him to change his grading methods. He stood his ground, and they eventually backed off. But the summer program was bringing more such interference even after promises from the administration that he would be calling the shots.

The program was small—just sixteen black students—and the majority were performing well. But a few weren't doing the required work, and Sowell worried that their presence would affect overall morale. His goal was to help the students who were there to learn, and he didn't want the ones who were acting out to be a distraction. He took the misbehaving students aside and told them to cut it out or leave, and in most cases that did the trick. But one participant refused to cooperate. He "was doing nothing—and doing it rather ostentatiously," and after the student ignored several warnings, Sowell told him he had to leave the program. The chairman of the economics department initially backed the decision, but then he changed his mind under pressure from colleagues and said the student must stay. "I was both astounded and furious," Sowell recalled. He and the chairman argued for nearly an hour. "Finally I said, 'You have my resignation—from the program and from Cornell University.'"[60]

The resignations were made to become effective at the end of the 1968–1969 academic year. Until then, Sowell continued to run the program and to teach. Several colleagues tried to convince him to reconsider, as did the Rockefeller Foundation, but his mind was made up. He had no more patience for the lies, the deceit, and the inclination among his peers to do the expedient thing instead of the right thing. Most of all, he was upset at how this affected the educational prospects of the students. For Sowell, black kids weren't window dressing for elite schools. He cared about their success, as he explained in his memoir:

> Now that my authority had been undermined, a degenerating atmosphere of non-cooperation and petty mischief developed in my class. Reports began coming in from other faculty members that students from this program were now absenting themselves from class for days, missing examinations, refusing to participate in class discussions and the like. Some were just goofing off, but others were no doubt responding to the racial militance of the regular Cornell black activists, who had contacted them, and who wanted "relevance" rather than a course taught like mine.
>
> The really dedicated students continued to do good work, but most students were in the uncertain middle between the single-minded workers and those who wanted to goof off or to go "relevant." This middle group was largely lost academically. Test scores in my course, which had been rising steadily, declined sharply. Similar results appeared in the students' other courses.[61]

In June 1969, eight months after Sowell had tendered his resignation, violent student riots erupted on Cornell's campus. Armed black militants, led by the school's Afro-American Society (AAS), seized control of the student activities center during a parents weekend and threatened the lives of people inside. The AAS had been created in 1966 by a group of black students who were heavily influenced by the Black Power movement. They were disrupting classes, occupying department offices, and physically threatening black and white students alike who wanted no part of their separatist agenda. Not only had all of this gone unpunished by Cornell, but some administrators had sided with the militants, which only encouraged more such behavior and led to increasingly strident demands. In a letter to the school paper, the AAS said that "if Blacks do not define the type of program set up within an institution that will be relevant to them, it will be worthless. Moreover, the Blacks must have the right to define the role of white students in the program, even to the point of their restriction, if it is to be valid for Blacks or whites."[62]

Sowell's worst fears were being realized. He'd warned against democratizing college campuses at all costs. He'd warned against accommodating student-determined "relevance." And he had predicted that racial double standards would be an educational disaster for blacks, that they would foster tension and resentment in the academy, and that they would turn otherwise bright students into campus revolutionaries brimming with grievances. He'd seen all of this coming, and now it had arrived. "In the spring of 1969," he wrote, "the guns-on-campus crisis made headlines: an armed occupation of a building, an agreement by the administration to meet sweeping demands, a repudiation of this agreement by the faculty, then threats by spokesmen for the armed black students if their demands were not met, and finally a humiliating reversal by the faculty."[63]

Technically, Sowell would remain in academia for another decade, but his last year at Cornell was pivotal. "I really lost whatever residual respect I had for the academic world that year," he told me. "When I came to Cornell, there would be parties at which people of all [ideological] persuasions would be present. The year I left that was no longer the case, even in the economics department. That's another thing that's happened since the 1960s." He would go on to teach economics at Brandeis University, Amherst College, and, finally, UCLA, where he received tenure. But throughout the 1970s he also spent several years away from the classroom. He headed research projects at the Urban Institute and the Center for Advanced Studies in Behavioral Sciences. And in addition to writing for scholarly journals about economics, he stepped up his writing for general audiences about race. He did pathbreaking work on black IQ scores and wrote a pioneering study of America's first black high school.[64] When he left Cornell, he didn't consider himself an expert on anything other than the history of economic thought. But he could write knowledgeably about what he had observed firsthand on the racial front, and he did. In 1969, he contributed an essay to a pamphlet about black studies programs edited by the civil rights activist Bayard Rustin. In 1970, he wrote a long essay about admissions policies for minority students for the *New York Times Magazine*. After it appeared, several publishers contacted him, and the result was his first book on a racial topic, *Black Education: Myths and Tragedies*, which appeared in 1972.

SOWELL OFFICIALLY LEFT TEACHING IN 1980 WHEN HE joined the Hoover Institution at Stanford University. The position came with no teaching obligations, which allowed him to focus entirely on his research and writing.

"I've studiously avoided entanglements with colleges for the past thirty-five years," he told me during an interview in 2015. "The most intolerant places you can be these days is the academic campus." Of course, we can only speculate about what would have happened had Sowell remained in academia. Friends, acquaintances, and others I spoke with who have followed his career are of two minds. Some imagine that if he had stuck it out, we would have many more intellectuals today who think like Thomas Sowell, given the thousands of graduate students who would have come in contact with him over the decades. But most argued that the trade-off would not have been worth it. Sowell has had a far larger impact, they said, through his books and columns, something that wouldn't have been possible if he had remained an academic economist with teaching responsibilities and also had to deal with the machinations of the faculty lounge.

"I doubt seriously if I would have written *Basic Economics* if I were still part of an economics department," Sowell told me. "People would have said, 'What the hell is Sowell doing writing a book about things any decently trained economist already knows? He's supposed to be advancing the frontiers of knowledge.'" *Basic Economics* has sold more copies than any other book he has written, but his fellow faculty members likely would have shrugged—or worse. "I remember at UCLA sitting among the senior faculty deciding the fate of a junior faculty member, reviewing contracts and granting tenure," he said. "And I remember one fellow being considered, and someone said he'd written a couple of very good textbooks. And then one of my colleagues said, 'I don't regard that as evidence of scholarship. I regard it as negative evidence of scholarship.'"[65]

George Gilder, who has known Sowell since the early 1980s and "edited" his 1981 book, *Markets and Minorities*—"You don't really edit Tom," he told me—said that it would be crazy to trade all the books and columns for more years of teaching. "How many books is it, thirty-something?" Gilder asked. "They're almost all in print. They're being read. They're influencing people around the world. He had a column for decades that was amazingly pithy and compelling. What I learned from Tom is how much you *lose* by succumbing to academic politics and the American academy, particularly at the highest levels in economics and social science, which is very corrupt."[66] What we know for certain is that Sowell's decision to stop giving it the old college try led to an astonishingly prolific career as a public intellectual. Even while still teaching in the 1970s he managed to publish five books. In the 1980s he would publish eight more, and then another eight in the 1990s—all in addition to writing a nationally syndicated weekly column. Professor Sowell had found a way to continue teaching outside of the classroom.

4

SOWELL'S RECONSIDERATIONS

"Retracing the footsteps of giants
not only makes us witnesses to the
intellectual clashes of the past, it adds
depth to our understanding of the ideas
that resulted from it all and which are
still with us today."[1]

IT'S ONE OF THE FUNNIER SCENES IN *SABRINA*, THE 1995 comedy starring Harrison Ford as a cranky, middle-aged tycoon named Linus Larrabee. When the daughter of the family's longtime chauffeur asks her father what Linus was like as a child, he gives a one-word answer: "Shorter." Like Linus, Thomas Sowell seems to have entered adolescence fully formed in key respects. He was already whip-smart, hyper-analytical, and supremely confident of his abilities. He was a contrarian who didn't much worry about burning his bridges. He was an independent thinker who welcomed rhetorical combat. And all of this was as obvious when Sowell was "shorter" as it was later in his life.

A middle-school teacher tried to discourage young Tommy from applying to one of New York City's most selective high schools because she didn't think he'd score well enough on the entrance exam. He ignored her advice and proceeded to score not only well enough to be admitted to the school, but high enough to be placed in honors classes. In the ninth grade, another teacher told him she was planning to submit an essay he'd written to a citywide contest: "She wanted to make some changes—I don't recall what—but she said that if she couldn't make them, then she couldn't send it in. I said, 'Then don't send it in.'"[2]

We don't know if the teachers took it personally, but we do know that Sowell would later think nothing of treating professors at Ivy League institutions and editors at major newspapers with the same high-handed indifference, for better or worse. "I still remember some officious copy editor at the *New York Times* saying that if I didn't accept some change in something I'd written, then it would be an inferior piece," he told me. "I said, 'No, it won't. Just put it in an envelope and send it back to me.'"[3] He once returned a book advance after the publisher insisted on changing dates in the manuscript to read AD 800 instead of 800 AD. "They said the correct form is AD 800, and I pointed out that various well-known university presses did it the other way. And then I said, 'You know, this is a very big book. And if we're going to go through it with this sort of Mickey Mouse stuff, it's not worth it.'"[4] They parted ways and he took the manuscript to another publisher, who paid him an even larger advance and had no problem with how the dates were written. Thinking back on these episodes, he wrote, "To say that my relationship with editors has not always been a happy one would be to completely understate the situation. To me, the fact that I have never killed an editor is proof that the death penalty deters."[5]

Sowell's senior honors thesis at Harvard was on the philosophy of Karl Marx, and one of the country's foremost authorities on Marxian economics at the time was Paul Sweezy, who had taught at Harvard and still lived in Cambridge. Sowell's thesis adviser offered to introduce him to Sweezy, who could offer guidance on organizing the paper and point him to reading material that an undergraduate student might ordinarily overlook. Sowell told the adviser not to bother with any introductions. His plan was "to ignore all interpreters of Marx, read right through the three volumes of *Capital*, and make up my own mind," he said. "I wasn't about to have anything I did attributed to ideas picked up from Paul Sweezy or anyone else."[6] The headstrong attitude was typical of Sowell, but so was the result. He graduated magna cum laude from Harvard, and parts of his senior thesis were later published in scholarly journals.

Sowell's willfulness even survived a two-year hitch in the Marines during the Korean War, when he regularly challenged superior officers and more than once came close to being court-martialed. "I was precisely the kind of wiseguy draftee they didn't like—and the wrong color on top of that," he later wrote. "As elsewhere throughout my life, I made enough enemies to get me in trouble and enough friends to get me out."[7] He would later butt heads with administrators while leading a research project at the Urban Institute in the 1970s. A colleague pulled him aside one day and said that to have any self-respect, he'd have to make it known that he was prepared to quit if necessary. "That was true at the Urban Institute and it was true elsewhere," said Sowell, who doesn't lack for self-awareness. "When I was teaching at Howard, it was leaked to me—I'm sure it was deliberate—that the dean had said that in all his years at Howard University, he had never encountered someone to whom he took such an instant and total dislike. I've apparently never been someone who brings us all together."[8]

Nor is he someone who is easily impressed or prone to trendy thinking. Today, Ta-Nehisi Coates is the black intellectual of the moment among liberal elites. In the early 1960s that distinction belonged to James Baldwin, the celebrated author and political activist whom Coates resembles somewhat in tone and prose style. In 1963, when Baldwin appeared on the cover of *Time* magazine, Sowell was teaching at Howard University and mystified by all the fuss that Baldwin's polemical essays were generating among the smart set. "Have been reading James Baldwin lately, and frankly I cannot see what all the shouting is about," he wrote to a friend. "It reminds me of a kid I knew in junior high school, who said a few bright things and was black, and therefore was a genius." Sowell didn't seem jealous of Baldwin's notoriety, just disappointed at what passed for deep thinking about race in America. He continued: "Baldwin can write with skill and certain poetic insights, but his talents do not include sustained analytical reasoning. He is, in short, well endowed in those areas where there is an oversupply already, and is badly lacking in the things that are needed to make a dent in the race problem. Baldwin gives emotional release to those who feel as he does, but it is hard to imagine that he will change anybody's mind."[9]

Sowell clearly had little use for protest writings in the mold of Baldwin. He understood that what was needed most when discussing fraught subjects such as race was sobriety, not histrionics, and that pushing people's buttons was not the same thing as advancing the conversation. But the letter also showed that long before Sowell himself became a public intellectual of any renown, he resisted automatically deferring to the supposed experts. The fact that Baldwin was an internationally famous literary heavyweight meant nothing, in and of itself. Rhetorical flourishes couldn't compensate for sloppy thinking. Sowell's early writings on economic history and his initial forays into racial controversies, which will be considered next, reflect not only his intellectual versatility but also his willingness to challenge the received wisdom of the present and the past. That willingness has defined his career, and it's born of a surpassing self-assurance that was there from the beginning.

IF TOM SOWELL CAME ACROSS IN HIS YOUTH AS SOMEONE wise beyond his years, for much of his adult life he physically resembled someone younger than his actual age. In 1981, not long after he had joined the Hoover Institution and was gaining more attention outside of academic circles, a *Washington Post* profile noted that he "looks not just young for 51, but extravagantly young. He has an utterly smooth face, a micro-pored brown which is unlined, untroubled, unqualmed by the attacks made on him for all these years. It's a face scarcely more worn than when it belonged to a little boy in Harlem."[10] Sowell had spent much of the previous decade building a reputation as a public intellectual. He was still teaching in the 1970s, but it's fair to say he had one foot out the classroom door. He testified before Congress about pending legislation.

He made his first appearance on a television talk show. He became a newspaper columnist. President Gerald Ford nominated him to the Federal Trade Commission, though Sowell ultimately decided to stay out of politics and withdrew his name from consideration. Mostly, however, it was a decade of research, writing, and broadening his intellectual horizons.

After releasing an undergraduate economics textbook in 1971, he published two books on the history of economics, *Say's Law: An Historical Analysis* (1972) and *Classical Economics Reconsidered* (1974). Unlike most of his later works, neither one was written for general readers. They featured original scholarship in his specialty, intellectual history, and they assumed a basic understanding of economics and a familiarity with technical language. They included graphs and equations and references that the average person would find difficult to follow. "Sismondi developed a theory of aggregate output equilibrium determined by a balancing of the declining utility of additional output and of the rising disutility of labor," reads a representative passage in *Classical Economics Reconsidered*.[11] But even in these earlier works we get glimpses of what would become the author's trademarks. Both books questioned orthodox thinking, and both included observations that other scholars' writing on the same subject had missed altogether or perhaps underplayed in significance.

"The classical economists are often depicted as defenders of the status quo, apologists for the socioeconomic powers (and practices) that be," he wrote in reference to prominent eighteenth- and nineteenth-century figures such as Adam Smith, Thomas Malthus, James Mill, and John Stuart Mill.[12] Sowell, however, believed that characterization was off base. He argued that their real concern was creating and sustaining economic growth to help the working class. He also said it would be more accurate to liken them to antiestablishment radicals, given how their laissez-faire theories challenged the thinking of landmark philosophers, including Plato and Machiavelli. The whole notion of a self-equilibrating system—the market economy—meant a diminished role for intellectuals and politicians. "In addition to opposing such major contemporary institutions as imperialism and slavery, the classical economists attacked the dominant social classes of the time: the landed aristocracy, the rising capitalists and the political powers."[13] And then we get this Sowellian insight: "One of the curious facts about the classical economists is that most of them were members of minority groups—minorities not simply in some numerical sense, but in ways that were socially relevant," he wrote. "Being a Scotsman was not an incidental fact in the England of Adam Smith's day. . . . Malthus, the two Mills, and J. R. McCulloch were also Scottish. David Ricardo was of Jewish ancestry and Jean-Baptiste Say was descended from Huguenots who had fled France during religious persecutions. Whatever their varying personal fortunes might be, these men were never full-fledged members of the establishment."[14]

In his book *Say's Law*, Sowell chronicled the development of and various controversies surrounding a concept that is foundational to classical economics. The doctrine gets its name from the French economist Jean-Baptiste Say, whose writings in the early nineteenth century helped popularize the works of Adam Smith throughout Europe and in the United States. In the wake of the industrial revolution, there was growing concern that the ability to produce so many more goods than before would outpace the ability of people to buy what was being produced, therefore resulting in large stockpiles of unsold goods and high levels of unemployment. Say was among those who argued that there was no need for a nation to worry about overproduction or underconsumption, because the total supply of goods would always equal the total demand for them. Say's Law, which states that "supply creates its own demand," is based on the premise that the very act of making things generates buying power equal to the value of what is being made.

The book was an expansion of Sowell's doctoral thesis, and he chose the topic over the strong objections of his mentor and dissertation committee chairman, George Stigler, who was widely recognized as the top scholar in the history of economic thought. Stigler, who would later be awarded the Nobel Prize in Economics, told Sowell that enough had already been written on the subject, and besides, he thought Sowell's interpretation was wrong. Of course, Sowell pressed on anyway, and by most accounts found something new and interesting to say. Reviewers credited him with writing "the first full-fledged history of the great controversies that Say's Law provoked," and praised his "mastery of elusive sources and the sustained power of critical analysis to which he subjects them."[15] *Say's Law* was a "desperately needed" book that "belongs on the shelves of all economists who are interested in the origins and development of their discipline."[16] It was yet another example of Sowell believing in himself, going his own way despite the warnings of others, and exceeding expectations.

In *Classical Economics Reconsidered*, Sowell extended his treatment of the origins of Say's Law and added an analysis of the historical development of several other major concepts in macroeconomic and microeconomic theory. He traced the clashes over these ideas among central intellectual figures, including Adam Smith, David Ricardo, and John Stuart Mill, and explained how their disputes sometimes resulted from evolving methodologies or simply different usage of the same terminology. Thomas Malthus and David Ricardo were close friends, for example, but they never settled on a common meaning of "supply" and "demand" in their economic writings. Sowell pointed out that these and other seemingly minor semantic quibbles complicated efforts to communicate clearly and build on the work of predecessors. "Definitions, as such, are neither 'right' nor 'wrong,'" he wrote, "but conflicting definitions made it difficult for these contemporaries to understand one another, or . . . to be understood by later interpreters."[17] This research impressed on Sowell the importance of writing with clarity and defining terms. Later in his career, he wrote that in his own work he strove to avoid ambiguity, especially when the subject matter was controversial: "Whether the reader will agree with all my conclusions is another question entirely. But disagreements can be productive, while misunderstandings seldom are."[18]

Like *Say's Law*, *Classical Economics Reconsidered* went over well with most critics. One reviewer described it as "a godsend"; another called it "a lively book by a real scholar—occasionally idiosyncratic, it is true, but a book by a man who knows his subject and who writes with vigour and with interest."[19] Again, these works were written primarily for serious students of economics, so unless mathematical models of general glut theory quicken your pulse, they're likely to be challenging reads.* But when Sowell chose to write in his field of expertise, he clearly excelled. These books showcased his considerable talents as both an economist and a historian, and his peers noticed. Years later, when the editors of the most prestigious reference work in economics, the *New Palgrave Dictionary of Economics*, were looking for someone to contribute definitive essays on Jean-Baptiste Say and Say's Law, they turned to Sowell, who was also chosen to write an entry on the scholarship of his old mentor George Stigler.[20]

A final note about these two early works: Although the word "reconsidered" appears in only one of the titles, both books are in fact reconsiderations of prior analyses. This was to become a hallmark of Sowell's scholarship. Sometimes it was explicit, as when he used similar phrasing in titles such as *Affirmative Action Reconsidered* (1975) and *Judicial Activism Reconsidered* (1989). Other times, it was more implicit but still abundantly clear that his intent was to challenge a prevailing "assumption" or "vision," or to

---

* In a textbook he later wrote for general readers, *Basic Economics: A Common Sense Guide to the Economy*, now in its fifth edition (2014), Sowell offered a remarkably cogent, jargon-free overview of the classical school and major figures in the history of economics. "Having written two textbooks on introductory economics—one full of graphs and equations, and the other with neither—I know from experience that the second way is a lot harder to write, and is more time-consuming," he explained. "The first book was written in a year; the second book took a decade." Thomas Sowell, "Teaching Economics," *Jewish World Review*, July 4, 2012, http://jewishworldreview.com /cols/sowell070412.php3#.XooAsIhKjIU.

offer what he considered to be a more accurate account of the past. But whether the subject was intellectual history, residential housing patterns, or language development in children, Sowell brought a certain skepticism of conventional theories to his analysis. He insisted on making up his own mind, which sometimes involved going back to square one and questioning the very framework that others had used to reach their conclusions. Historical revisionists who interpret past events to fit a certain ideology deserve derision. But Sowell had a different goal, which was to guard against misreading the past and formulating policies based on propositions that are no longer true or perhaps never were. As the prominent historian James McPherson explained, "revision is the lifeblood of historical scholarship. History is a continuing dialogue between the present and the past. Interpretations of the past are subject to change in response to new evidence, new questions asked of the evidence, new perspectives gained by the passage of time."[21] Sowell distinguished himself as a scholar by taking nothing for granted and seeking answers to questions that others had long stopped bothering to ask.

SOWELL WOULD RETURN TO WRITING ABOUT HIS SPECIALTY from time to time throughout his career. He published a book on Marxism in 1985, and an expanded version of *Classical Economics Reconsidered*, titled *On Classical Economics*, in 2006. But for the balance of the 1970s his attention was elsewhere. In 1972 he published the semi-autobiographical *Black Education: Myths and Tragedies*, which grew out of a long essay he had written for the *New*

York Times Magazine after leaving Cornell. And in 1975 he released *Race and Economics*, a book that covered several themes he would return to repeatedly over the next four decades, including migration, the historical experiences of various ethnic groups, and the government's role in their economic advancement.

The idea of applying economic principles to racial issues came to Sowell through Benjamin Rogge, a professor of economics at Wabash College in Indiana. In the late 1960s, when Sowell was teaching at Cornell, Rogge visited the school to give a talk titled "The Welfare State Against the Negro." Sowell was traveling at the time and missed the event, but he later contacted Rogge to ask him about his research and the two became friends. Rogge was writing a book on the subject but never got around to finishing it. Eventually, he "took his manuscript and simply handed it to me and said do with it whatever you can," Sowell told me. "I was flabbergasted. I don't think I ever used anything directly from his manuscript. But the fundamental idea that you could apply economics to racial issues—that was the inspiration."[22]

Another inspiration for *Race and Economics* was Nathan Glazer and Daniel Patrick Moynihan's 1963 study of ethnic behavior, *Beyond the Melting Pot*. Future books by Sowell, such as *Ethnic America* (1981) and *The Economics and Politics of Race* (1983), would delve more deeply into the social and economic significance of cultural patterns. His research in this area would culminate with the publication of his 1990s trilogy: *Race and Culture* (1994), *Migrations and Culture* (1996), and *Conquests and Culture*

(1998). But *Race and Economics* offered peeks of what was to come.*

The book also had a significant impact on a young attorney in the Midwest named Clarence Thomas, who independently had reached similar conclusions about racial inequality but was unaware of other blacks who shared his viewpoint. He would later write that the "absence of dissenting black voices" in discussions of race in America "was so complete that I found it hard at times not to doubt

---

* Sowell told me that he ultimately "became dissatisfied" with *Race and Economics* and declined several offers to have it reprinted. "There were some errors in it," he said, citing as an example the book's discussion of slavery: "I accepted the notion that slaves were treated better in Latin America on the grounds that there were more laws in Latin America safeguarding slaves. The fallacy is that it doesn't matter what the law says. What matters is what actually happens, and what actually happened is that slaves were treated better in the [US] South for economic reasons." He elaborated: "The incentives facing the slave overseer are different from the incentives facing the slave owner. The slave overseer has the incentive to get the maximum output during his tenure, not only to keep his job but also to say, after he moves on, 'I got so many bales of cotton per person. . . .' The slave owner owns not simply the current output but the future economic value of the slaves. And so if a slave overseer works the slave past the optimum point, then the long-run damage is sustained economically by the owner. . . . In the Caribbean the slave owner probably lived in London. In the United States, the slave owner probably lived on the plantation. And so, for example, pregnant women were given more time off in the United States than in the Caribbean, and the infant mortality rate was several times higher in the Caribbean than in the United States. There were economic incentives to do things that are sometimes more effective than legal protections. So, I don't repudiate the fundamental theme of [*Race and Economics*], but future books supersede it while incorporating from it whatever was worth incorporating."

my own convictions." Then he read a review of *Race and Economics* in the *Wall Street Journal*. "I felt like a thirsty man gulping down a glass of cool water," he recalled. "Here was a black man who was saying what I thought—and not behind closed doors, either, but in the pages of a book that has just been reviewed in a national newspaper. Never before had I seen my views stated with such crisp, unapologetic clarity: the problems faced by blacks in America would take quite some time to solve, and the responsibility for solving them would fall largely on black people themselves."[23]

By the mid-1970s, it was clear that Sowell could do something that is rare among academics. He not only wrote with authority but also in a manner that was engaging and accessible to nonexperts. "He is extremely empirical—that's what he does," said Fred Barnes, the veteran political journalist. "Even in an 800- or 900-word column, he'll offer empirical ideas or empirical data to make his case. It's not just sheer opinion. There are not many other [columnists] who do that. As I think about it, nobody else writes like that. One of the reasons is that he knows a lot more."[24]

Newspaper and magazine editors took notice, and Sowell began writing more frequently for general-interest publications, particularly on racial topics. Irving Kristol, editor of the quarterly publication *The Public Interest*, invited Sowell to a dinner party in the early 1970s, and the two men got into a discussion about black education. When Kristol asked what could be done to create high-quality schools for blacks, Sowell replied that such schools already existed and had for generations. This was news to Kristol, who persuaded Sowell to write about them for the magazine. A 1974 issue of *The Public Interest* featured a lengthy essay by Sowell on the history of all-black Dunbar High School in Washington, DC, which had outperformed its local white counterparts and repeatedly equaled or exceeded national norms on standardized tests throughout the first half of the twentieth century. Over an eighty-five-year span, from 1870 to 1955, the piece noted, "most of Dunbar's graduates went on to college, even though most Americans—white or black—did not."[25] Two years later, in the same publication, he wrote a second article on successful black elementary and high schools in the United States. Sowell later told a friend that his work on black education had been "the most emotionally satisfying research I have ever done."[26]

But the research also raised serious questions about public policy. The Supreme Court had ruled, in its 1954 decision *Brown v. Board of Education*, that racially segregated schools were "inherently unequal," and that separating black and white children impaired the ability of black students to learn. If that was true, however, what explained the success of Dunbar High School, which was located just blocks away from the building where the Supreme Court decision was handed down? Had court-ordered busing policies, aimed at achieving racial balance in the classroom, really been necessary? Or should the focus all along have been on creating quality schools in every neighborhood, regardless of their racial makeup? More fundamentally, Sowell was bothered by the fact that there was so little interest, including among his fellow black scholars, in studying the academically rigorous black schools that did exist, and trying to replicate what had made them so successful.

"While Irving Kristol was very interested in how first-rate education had been achieved in a black school, no one in the black establishment seemed at all interested, except for a few who tried to discredit the results by saying that Dunbar was a middle-class school for the sons and daughters of doctors and lawyers," said Sowell. "My data showed that there were far more Dunbar students whose mothers were maids than there were students whose fathers were doctors." His takeaway from the experience was that "black 'leaders' had a preconceived agenda," and they were "opposed to whatever retarded that agenda. In education, the agenda was racial integration in general, including busing. Discussions of first-rate all-black schools were a distraction from that agenda."[27]

SOWELL TOOK A SIMILARLY IDIOSYNCRATIC APPROACH TO the nature-versus-nurture debate over race and intelligence. In a research project he directed at the Urban Institute from 1972 to 1974, he and his colleagues collected more than seventy thousand intelligence-test records from individuals representing a dozen different ethnic and racial groups going back a half-century. At the time, the most prominent proponent of the view that intelligence was mostly hereditary was Arthur Jensen, an educational psychologist at the University of California at Berkeley. In 1969, Jensen had published a controversial academic article saying that blacks had lower IQs than whites, primarily as a result of genetics, and that compensatory education programs aiming to close the learning gap, such as Head Start, would inevitably fail.[28] An uproar ensued, and Jensen was roundly denounced as a racist crank. He started receiving death threats and needed bodyguards when he appeared in public forums. His detractors argued that environmental and cultural factors, not genes, explained the racial disparity in IQ scores, calling for an end to the use of intelligence testing, achievement testing, and standardized testing altogether.

Sowell didn't care that this was a taboo subject, and he ignored warnings from prominent black scholars to steer clear of it.[29] He wasn't fearful of what he might find or worried that responding to genetic intelligence theories might help legitimize them. Sowell wasn't interested in name-calling, either. He was skeptical, but he also regarded Jensen as a serious scholar who deserved an intelligent rebuttal that went beyond public shaming and ad hominem dismissals. "I'd read Jensen's article that started all this, and I saw this work of scholarship, but I wasn't convinced," he told me. "Partly, just from personal experience. I compared the understanding of black people that I knew with virtually no education with some of the smug shallowness I encountered at Harvard. Then I said to myself, 'I'm 90 percent certain that Jensen is wrong. But what about the other 10 percent? What if I do find out if there's a difference?'" He concluded that exploring the matter was worth the risk: "I've always believed that the facts were so fundamental—that wherever you want to go, literally or figuratively, you can only get there from where you are. If you want to do the best you can do for someone, you had to know where they are in reality."[30]

Sowell's research wound up unveiling a number of reasons to doubt Jensen's theory that racial differences in average IQ scores were innate. There were white groups in the United States and elsewhere with IQ scores similar to those of blacks, for example. There were black schools with student IQ scores exceeding the national average. And black women, it turned out, were significantly overrepresented among people with high IQs.[31] Jensen's theories of genetic determinism couldn't explain these outcomes. Nor could they explain studies that showed black orphans raised by white families having an average IQ of 106 at a time when the average score of blacks nationally was 85 and the average score of whites was 100.[32]

At the same time, Sowell suspected that Jensen's detractors were also overstating *their* case. "Jensen starts with the premise that there is a unique black I.Q. which has a unique genetic explanation," he said in a 1980 interview. "The critics start from the premise that there is a unique environmental explanation. Neither of them has raised the more basic question: Is there in fact a unique black I.Q.? And that is why I did the historical study. The answer I found was that no, there is not." Sowell explained how the empirical evidence undermined both theories:

If you go back around 1910, 1920, you will find a great number of groups who had IQs the same or lower than the IQs of blacks. What you find is that as most of those groups rose socially and economically, their IQs rose. So that you had, for example, Polish IQs that were the same level as blacks around World War I; now Polish IQs are above the national average. Jews, very surprisingly, scored quite low in mental tasks during World War I, and in fact the man who invented the college boards—SAT—said that we have now disproved the popular notion that Jews are intelligent. His proof was somewhat premature, we found out, and Jews have won about a quarter of all Nobel Prizes won by Americans.[33]

Those who wanted to ban such testing—then often called "mental testing"—believed that comparisons between groups had no use other than to feed racist theories, but Sowell disagreed. Just because these results could be misused didn't mean they should be discarded altogether. These tests, Sowell noted, had accurately predicted future performance. They weren't flawless, but they had been shown empirically to be better predictors of outcomes than other kinds of tests and provided an objective way to assess the performance of school systems. "Every educational program will always be a 'success' as judged by those who run it," so a "concern for children's mental development requires that there be independent tests as well. It is not mental testing that needs to be stopped, but the blind worship or blind hostility with which different people react to it."[34] Sowell argued that disadvantaged minorities especially benefited from testing because, as past studies had shown, subjective analyses were more likely to overlook gifted students who were black. In other words, nixing the tests altogether in the interest of avoiding bias could be counterproductive: "If biased people use mental tests to discriminate, eliminating the test will not eliminate the bias. Objective tests at least put some limits on their bias."[35]

Before publishing a scholarly response to Jensen's research in his 1978 book, *Essays and Data on American Ethnic Groups*, Sowell summarized his findings in an article for the *New York Times Magazine*. His point was not that genetic heritage played no role in a person's mental capability, but that social and economic progress seemed to matter more. He also stressed that a racial or ethnic group's intelligence wasn't fixed in place forever and could rise significantly within a few generations. This historical pattern had been observed among European and Asian minority groups in the twentieth century, both in the United States and in other countries. What mattered more than genes was cultural assimilation and economic advancement. "For groups with upward mobility, there has been a marked rise in I.Q.'s over time," he wrote. "The average I.Q.'s of Italian-Americans and Polish-Americans have risen by 20 to 25 points from the time of the surveys conducted around World War I to the surveys conducted in the 1970s. This rise is greater than the current I.Q. difference—about 15 points—between blacks and whites."[36] He predicted that it was "likely" that black and Hispanic IQ scores would rise as those groups progressed socioeconomically. And sure enough, a study of black cognitive ability released in 2006 by the social scientists William Dickens and James Flynn concluded that blacks had gained as many as seven IQ points on whites since the early 1970s.[37]

After Jensen read the *Times* article, he contacted Sowell and they met for lunch. Jensen told Sowell that it was the strongest rebuttal to his research that he had read. "He really was part of an old-fashioned sense of scholarship," Sowell said. "He wasn't trying to convince me one way or the other. He wanted to know what the evidence was. Years later—maybe fifteen years later—I was surprised one day to see a letter from Jensen saying that his latest research showed a small increase in the average IQ of blacks. No indication that he'd changed his position, but . . . he wanted to be sure that the knowledge—the information on all sides—was out there."[38]

In 1994, Richard Herrnstein and Charles Murray published their book *The Bell Curve* to reviews that were, if anything, even more antagonistic than what Jensen had experienced twenty-five years earlier. The book is about intelligence tests, not race, but it does cite Jensen's theories favorably. Herrnstein, a professor of psychology at Harvard, died shortly before the book was released; Murray is a scholar at the American Enterprise Institute who first distinguished himself through his writings on welfare policy in the 1980s. Sowell wrote a 3,600-word review of *The Bell Curve* for the politically conservative *American Spectator* magazine.[39] He praised the authors for exposing the flaws in arguments about intelligence testing being "culturally biased" and not accurately predicting future performance. And he defended Herrnstein and Murray against critics who were more interested in questioning their motives than their data. When it came to the book's discussion of a genetic basis for racial differences in IQ scores, however, Sowell was just as merciless in picking apart the authors' conclusions as he was in dealing with Jensen's in the 1970s.

To its credit, wrote Sowell, *The Bell Curve* accurately presented the evidence against the authors' claims about heredity and intelligence. The problem was that Herrnstein and Murray "seem not to see how crucially" that evidence "undermines the case for a genetic explanation of interracial IQ differences." Average IQ scores had risen over time even though the authors hypothesized that they would fall as a result of higher fertility rates among lower-IQ groups. As significantly, the variance in IQ scores within racial and ethnic groups was larger than the variance between them:

> The failure to draw the logical inference seems puzzling. Blacks today are just as racially different from whites of two generations ago as they are from whites of today. Yet the data suggest that the number of questions that blacks answer correctly on IQ tests is very similar to the number answered correctly by past generations of whites. If race A differs from race B in IQ, and two generations of race A differ from each other by the same amount, where is the logic in suggesting that the IQ differences are racial, even partially?
>
> Herrnstein and Murray do not address this question . . .[40]

Sowell also had a more fundamental problem with the book and went so far as to question the rigor of its scholarship. "Perhaps the most troubling aspect of *The Bell Curve* from an intellectual standpoint is the authors' uncritical approach to statistical correlation," he wrote. "One of the first things taught in introductory statistics is that correlation is not causation. It is also one of the first things forgotten and one of the most widely ignored facts in public policy research."[41]

The point here is not to rehash the testing debate. Rather, it is to further illustrate Sowell's independent thinking and maverick inclinations. Clearly, he didn't hesitate to criticize even his fellow travelers on the political right when he felt it was warranted. Charles Murray has been an A-list conservative for four decades, and on other issues

Sowell has cited his work favorably, both before and after the release of *The Bell Curve*. Their agreements may far outweigh their disagreements, but that didn't stop Sowell from offering a highly critical analysis of the book. What mattered more to Sowell was whether an individual's arguments could withstand scrutiny, not how the individual identified politically or ideologically, and he refused to pull his punches even when dealing with other conservatives.

Sowell has gotten little credit for this principled behavior, especially among black liberals, who prefer to caricature him as someone forever in search of white approval, no matter that his track record says otherwise. The reality is that Sowell criticized Ronald Reagan's decision in 1980 to give a campaign speech defending states' rights in the small city of Philadelphia, Mississippi, where three civil rights workers had been abducted and murdered in 1964.[42] The reality is that although Milton Friedman was his former professor, mentor, and friend, Sowell consistently— and publicly—opposed Friedman's negative income-tax proposals to address poverty.[43] The reality is that he has quarreled with libertarians over foreign military intervention as well as with neoconservative advocates of "nation-building."[44] Sowell has shown time and again over the decades that he is his own man, even when it meant ruffling the feathers of ideological allies.

As was the case with Jensen, Murray and Sowell would remain on friendly terms. When I spoke to Murray about Sowell's career, he offered only praise, particularly with regard to the latter's ability to convey important concepts and ideas to the general public. "Back in the 1970s, how many people were there who were serious academics who were saying these things? There must have been people besides Milton Friedman and Tom Sowell, but there weren't very many," Murray said. "Tom was one of the very few . . . who was writing things that I had to take seriously, just because of the nature of the writing and the evidence and the rest of it," he added. Other economists he respected, such as George Stigler and Gary Becker, were active as well, but "Stigler was not a household name and neither was Becker. Tom and Milton got books out there that were intended for a broader audience and got a broader audience, which I think was crucial in resurrecting just awareness of classical liberal principles."

Then Murray mentioned another name: "And, of course, there was Hayek, who was also being published around that same time. But even Hayek, in the United States, didn't get the exposure, I think, that Tom and Milton did." Murray was referring to the Austrian economist Friedrich Hayek, who is widely known for his 1944 polemic on the dangers of socialism, *The Road to Serfdom*. The US publisher initially printed just two thousand copies, which sold out almost immediately, and a second printing began within a week. It was reviewed on the front page of the *New York Times Book Review* by noted economic journalist Henry Hazlitt, who described *The Road to Serfdom* as "one of the most important books of our generation," likening its "power and rigor of reasoning" to that on display in *On Liberty*, John Stuart Mill's landmark nineteenth-century essay on the importance of individual freedom and sovereignty.[45] Within a few months, *The Road to Serfdom* had become so popular that *Reader's Digest*, the largest-circulation periodical in the country at the time, ran a twenty-page abridged version, and the Book-of-the-Month Club distributed more than a million reprints. A book by an Austrian émigré intended for his fellow intellectual elites had become the unlikeliest of American best sellers. Hayek was awarded the 1974 Nobel Prize in Economics, but he also made significant contributions in the fields of political philosophy and social theory.

Between 1950 and 1962, Hayek taught at the University of Chicago—and one of his students was Thomas Sowell. Nearly two decades after taking Hayek's course in the history of economic thought, Sowell would publish *Knowledge and Decisions*, a book that was inspired by Hayek's own scholarship and that would change the course of Sowell's career.

5

SOWELL'S KNOWLEDGE

"Some of the biggest cases of mistaken
identity are among intellectuals who
have trouble remembering that they are
not God."[1]

IN THE FINAL CHAPTER OF HIS MEMOIR, *A PERSONAL ODYSSEY*,
Sowell wrote that he "grew up with no fear of whites,
either physically or intellectually," and explained how that
mindset later influenced his scholarship. Leaving North
Carolina as a young child and growing up in New York
City during the 1930s and 1940s were happenstances.
But given his strong-willed personality, Sowell believed
that quitting Dixie was a key factor in his development as
an intellectual and set him apart from many of his black
contemporaries. "Had I remained in the South, such fear
might have become necessary for survival in adulthood,
assuming that I would have survived," he wrote. "But fear
is all too often the enemy of rational thought. Many blacks
during the 1960s (and later) were inordinately impressed
with strident loudmouths whose chief claim was that they
'stood up to the white man.' . . . I was never really impressed

by such credentials—and certainly did not regard them as a substitute for knowing what you are talking about."[2]

When I asked Sowell to elaborate on that passage during one of our conversations, he said, "I think that's why people like Malcolm X made such an impact, because he wasn't fearful. This is one of the reasons people are so ferocious against people like [Arthur] Jensen and [Charles] Murray" and others who have speculated about race and intelligence. "They are afraid in a sense that I'm not." Thinking back to his childhood, he recalled being added to a class in junior high school for students with IQs of 120 and above, which put them around the 95th percentile. "After the first math exam the teacher said that only one person got a hundred on it, and he was thumbing through the papers trying to find it. And being in a funny mood, I said, 'Thomas Sowell?' And he said, 'Yes, that's the name.'" Sowell didn't make much of it at the time, "but I think that was enormously significant for my future. It meant from that moment on, there was no reason for any white in that class to think that he was superior. And there was no reason for me to be worried about competing."[3]

Sowell's admirers never tire of noting his bravery, by which they usually mean his willingness to challenge the black civil rights orthodoxy and take controversial positions on any number of issues surrounding social inequality. That sort of praise is understandable and certainly warranted, but it's also much too limiting. Sowell's iconoclasm extends beyond his opposition to affirmative action programs and minimum wage laws. He's made those arguments as well as anyone and better than most. But his legacy is more than that. Viewed in its totality, his scholarship showcases a willingness to grapple with some of our most enduring philosophical questions: how knowledge is developed, how justice and injustice are defined, how basic conceptions of human nature differ and have led to contrasting political theories going back more than two centuries.

It was to these issues that Sowell turned his attention in the mid-1970s as he began transitioning away from academia and toward public intellectualism. He took a break from teaching at UCLA to become a Fellow at Stanford University's Center for Advanced Study in the Behavioral Sciences, where he began research on a book about how societies produce and process information. This was an entirely new intellectual challenge for Sowell, whose scholarly output until then had focused mainly on writing about economic history and race. The end product, titled *Knowledge and Decisions*, would become his most ambitious book yet, and it would help facilitate something he had been contemplating for close to a decade: the end of his teaching career.

As a graduate student at the University of Chicago, Sowell had enrolled in a class on the history of ideas taught by Friedrich Hayek. A paper on Say's Law that he wrote for the course received high praise from the professor and was later published in a British academic journal. But it was Sowell's introduction to Hayek's own writings, by way of Milton Friedman, that would prove far more consequential. Sowell took Friedman's mandatory price theory course at Chicago and was assigned to read an article titled "The Use of Knowledge in Society," which Hayek had published in a 1945 issue of the *American Economic Review*. Hayek's seminal essay concerned how societies function (or malfunction) through the spread of the information that people use to make economic decisions. His central insight was that knowledge is widely dispersed—no one person or group of people can possibly know everything—so, if a society's resources are to be allocated efficiently, it follows that the decision-making process ought to be decentralized as well. "The knowledge of the circumstances of which we must make use never exists in a concentrated or integrated form, but solely as the dispersed bits of incompletely and frequently contradictory knowledge which all the separate individuals possess," Hayek wrote.

Essentially, it was an argument against centrally planned economies, where a few people make decisions on behalf of everyone, and in favor of market-based economies, where prices determined by supply and demand convey the relevant information that allows individuals to make decisions for themselves. Because different people have different needs, and those needs are constantly changing, it is impossible for government planners to keep track of what to produce, or in what quantities, and at what price to produce it. "The economic problem of society is thus not merely a problem of how to allocate 'given' resources," wrote Hayek. "It is rather a problem of how to secure the best use of resources known to any of the members of society, for ends whose relative importance only these individuals know."

Hayek described two distinct kinds of knowledge that people possess. One is "scientific knowledge," by which he meant theoretical or technical expertise. The other is "unorganized knowledge," which is peculiar to each person's situation. It's what you know about your own situation as well as the "local conditions" and "special circumstances" of the people around you. Hayek said that it is with respect to this second kind of knowledge that "practically every individual has some advantage over all others," even the experts, because no one knows your circumstances better than you do. The problem with central planning is that, however intelligent those in charge may be, they're not omniscient, and thus they lack this localized awareness of the specific wants and needs unique to each individual. "If we can agree that the economic problem in society is mainly one of rapid adaptation to changes in the particular circumstances of time and place, it would seem to follow that the ultimate decisions must be left to the people who are familiar with these circumstances, who know directly of the relevant changes and of the resources immediately available to meet them," Hayek wrote. "We cannot expect that this problem will be solved by first communicating all this knowledge to a central board which, after integrating all knowledge, issues its orders. We must solve it by some form of decentralization."

To illustrate the point, Hayek used the example of market competition for products that use tin. If there's a shortage of available tin, we'll find out soon enough, because the price of the metal and the products containing it will increase. The average person may not know or understand the precise reason for the shortage, but people will nevertheless adjust their behavior accordingly by using less tin and finding substitutes. "The whole acts as one market, not because any of its members survey the whole field, but because their limited individual fields of vision sufficiently overlap so that through many intermediaries the relevant information is communicated to all," wrote Hayek. "The marvel is that . . . without an order being issued, without more than perhaps a handful of people knowing the cause, tens of thousands of people whose identity could not be ascertained by months of investigation, are made to use the material or its products more sparingly; that is, they move in the right direction."[4]

HAYEK WAS EXPANDING ON THE IDEAS OF HIS MENTOR, fellow Austrian economist Ludwig von Mises, and on predecessors, such as Adam Smith, who theorized that individuals acting in their own economic self-interest ultimately promote the interests of society as a whole. Where Smith stressed the importance of the division of labor in the marketplace, Hayek emphasized the division of knowledge. In *Knowledge and Decisions*, Sowell would expand on Hayek's insights, and he would do so in ways that even Hayek had never contemplated. The "spark" for the book was Hayek's three-page essay in the *American Economic Review*.

"Initially, it made no impression on me," Sowell said. "I just wondered why Friedman had assigned it for a PhD course on price theory." It was only after Sowell had left Chicago and accepted his first academic post that he came to fully appreciate the article's significance: "When I started teaching at Douglass College, because I had written stuff about Marx . . . they thought I should teach a course on the Soviet economy. There's no real connection, but I had to go cram on the Soviet economy." The research took his mind back to graduate school. "As I went through all this stuff, I ran across all kinds of puzzling anomalies in the Soviet economy that then forced me to think back to Hayek's essay. I could see what the factors were that led the Soviets to do what they were doing, and why it wasn't working. There was a knowledge problem that was inherent in that system. In a nutshell, those with the power didn't have the knowledge, and those with the knowledge didn't have the power."[5]

Sowell initially intended for *Knowledge and Decisions* to be around two hundred pages long, but as he added more practical examples—one economist later called them "metaphors in technicolor"—to build on its central thesis, the manuscript swelled to more than double that size. The Hayek article "really sort of gave me a set of questions to ask," he said in an interview with *Reason* magazine shortly after the book was published. "It was not just the elucidation of a principle that was important. It was the fact that, with this thought in the back of my mind, I saw many, many things that fit into this pattern. I was just amazed at all the very different kinds of situations in which you have this basic problem: How do you get the knowledge from the person who knows to the person who makes the decision? And particularly, how do you get it to him in a form that gets him to make the right decision?"[6]

Knowledge and Decisions is a serious and sometimes demanding work that aims to deepen the reader's understanding of a big topic: how prices serve as communication mechanisms in a society, and thus help people adjust over time to dynamic conditions in the real world. But Sowell also took pains to write in a style more accessible than Hayek's because he hoped to reach an audience far wider than the narrow readership of the *American Economic Review*. In lieu of graphs and equations he offers rich metaphors and copious real-world examples that make the weightier concepts under discussion not merely digestible but tasty. Here he is in an early passage describing how raw information becomes knowledge:

> Physicists have determined that even the most solid and heavy mass of matter we see is mostly empty space. But at the submicroscopic level, specks of matter scattered through a vast emptiness have such incredible density and weight, and are linked to one another by such powerful forces, that together they produce all the properties of concrete, cast iron and solid rock. In much the same way, specks of knowledge are scattered through a vast emptiness of ignorance, and everything depends upon how solid the individual specks of knowledge are, and how powerfully linked and coordinated they are with one another. The vast spaces of ignorance do not prevent the specks of knowledge from forming a solid structure, though sufficient *misunderstanding* can disintegrate it in much the same way that radioactive atomic structures can disintegrate (uranium into lead) or even explode.[7]

The first half of the book concerns the very nature of knowledge—how it is created from ideas, authenticated through feedback mechanisms, and then applied in decision-making. How is it possible that humans can "perform intricate functions requiring enormous knowledge" when "individually we know so pathetically little"?[8] Sowell's answer is that we've created formal and informal "decision-making units" to evaluate these dispersed bits of knowledge and determine what is or isn't useful. These units include families, customs, religions, political parties, governments, and other systems and institutions that are too numerous to name. And the different kinds of decisions that these units help us make each day are just as varied:

> For example, some decisions are *binary* decisions—yes or no, war or peace, guilty or innocent—while other decisions are *continuously variable* incremental decisions: using more or less gasoline, paying higher or lower wages, living a more relaxed or more hectic life. Some decisions are once-and-for-all decisions—suicide, loss of virginity, burning a Rembrandt painting—while others are readily reversible decisions: turning off a television program that is not interesting, cancelling a subscription, ceasing to purchase a given brand of consumer goods or ceasing to use certain clichés, etc. Decisions may also be made individually or as "package deals." One can buy onions, bread, and canned goods in the same store or in different stores, but in choosing between political candidates, one must choose one candidate's whole package—his fiscal policy, environmental position, foreign policy, civil liberties views, etc.—as against the whole package of his opponent's positions on the same subjects.[9]

Sowell goes on to examine decision-making in three major areas: economics, politics, and the law. And while the processes of verifying and utilizing information can differ considerably from one institution to the next, Sowell was more interested in exploring what they have in common. Regardless of the institution, choices are constrained—by time, resources, or some other limitation—which means that decision-making necessarily involves trade-offs, or weighing one option against another. "While the crucial question for social decision-making processes is the impact of those processes on society as a whole, attempts to answer that question cannot automatically proceed as if society as a whole is the decision-making unit," he wrote. "Rather, what must be considered are the incentives and constraints facing the actual decision makers, in order to determine if their decisions are likely to produce socially optimal results."[10] His point was that what matters most is who gets to make the decision: "The most basic question is not what is best but *who shall decide* what is best."[11]

The balance of the book details contemporary trends. Sowell's worry was that, over time, the ultimate decision maker has become increasingly more distant and remote from the individuals or entities most directly affected by whatever is decided. The authority to make decisions had moved away from those decentralized and intimate makeshift units and toward third-party individuals and institutions that lacked experience or training or any personal stake in a given outcome. "Even within democratic nations, the locus of decision making has drifted away from the individual, the family, and voluntary associations of various sorts, and toward government," he wrote. "And within government, it has moved away from elected officials subject to voter feedback, and toward more insulated government institutions, such as bureaucracies and the appointed judiciary. These trends have grave implications, not only for individual freedom, but also for the social ways in which knowledge is used, distorted, or made ineffective."[12]

THESE TRENDS, HE ARGUED, HAVE BEEN EXACERBATED BY the rise in prominence and power of intellectuals, who "have spearheaded criticisms of price-coordinated decision making," or capitalism, and who as far back as polls and voting records have been kept have been "well to the political left of the general population."[13] The underlying problem is not that these intellectual elites—which include not only academics but also journalists, social activists, and others who produce and disseminate ideas—tend to be more liberal than the surrounding society. Rather, the problem is that they are uncritically accepted as independent authorities offering disinterested advice on this or that issue: "It is not so much the bias of 'expert' intellectuals that is crucial, but the *difference* between their perceived 'objective' expertise and the reality which makes the political process vulnerable to their influence."

Ideally, intellectuals would be viewed as just another special interest group that competes with others in the process of reaching a decision. Yet the ability of the intellectual class to present itself as a nonideological servant of the public good has given it outsized and unwarranted influence. "Publicly recognized special interest groups—landlords discussing rent control, oil companies discussing energy, etc.—may have similar incentives and constraints, but are far less effective in getting their social viewpoints accepted as objective truth," wrote Sowell. "But when an academic intellectual appears as an 'expert' witness before a congressional committee, no one ever asks if he has been a recipient of large research grants or lucrative consulting fees from the very agency whose programs he is about to 'objectively' assess in terms of the public interest."[14]

In later books, including *The Vision of the Anointed,*
The Quest for Cosmic Justice, and *Intellectuals and Society,* Sowell would tackle the history and merits of specific
policies promoted by public intellectuals. Here, his primary
concern was the expanding role of experts in politics. Intellectuals tend to favor less reliance on the market and more
reliance on centralized government, which translates into
less efficient applications of knowledge and a larger gap
between the people who make decisions and those who
have to live with the consequences. Sowell stressed that
intellectuals stay relevant to the decision-making process
by convincing nonintellectuals that their own knowledge
is inadequate:

> An intellectual is rewarded not so much for reaching the truth as for demonstrating his own mental
> ability. Recourse to well-established and widely accepted ideas will never demonstrate the mental ability of the intellectual, however valid its application
> to a particular question or issue. The intellectual's
> virtuosity is shown by recourse to the new, the esoteric, and if possible his own originality in concept
> or application—whether or not its conclusions are
> more or less valid than the received wisdom. Intellectuals have an incentive "to study more the reputation of their own wit than the success of another's
> business," as [Thomas] Hobbes observed more than
> three centuries ago.[15]

Sowell cautioned against losing sight of the fact that
intellectuals as a group have occupational self-interests just
like everyone else. They labor to convince others that the

kind of knowledge that narrowly trained scholars possess is the most important kind, which serves to "increase the demand for intellectuals by discrediting alternatives."[16] In Sowell's view, the discord between public opinion and the policy preferences of intellectuals has steadily worsened. Moreover, an intelligentsia that once perceived the average citizen in a liberal democracy as an ally now regards "public opinion and democratic processes as obstacles to overcome." His fear was that the rising influence of the intellectual class in political decision-making would inevitably lead to less freedom in society overall. "The characteristics of the intellectual vision are strikingly similar to the characteristics of totalitarian ideology," he explained, "especially the localization of evil and of wisdom and the psychic identification with the interests of great masses, whose actual preferences are ignored in favor of the overriding preferences of intellectuals."[17]

Today, the belief in "social justice" as a moral imperative has become all the rage, and its jargon—"white privilege," "systemic racism," "unconscious bias"—has entered the media lexicon. But Sowell saw the country bounding in this direction decades ago and noted the trade-offs:

> More justice for all is a contradiction in terms, in a world of diverse values and disparate conceptions of justice itself. "More" justice in such a world means more forcible imposition of one particular brand of justice—i.e., less freedom. Perfect justice in this context means perfect tyranny. The point is not merely semantic or theoretical. The reach of national political power into every nook and cranny has proceeded in step with campaigns for greater "social justice."[18]

And then we get a real-world example—the Chicago school touch—to drive home the point: "A parent forced by the law and income to send his child off to a public school where he is abused or terrorized by other children is painfully aware of a loss of freedom, however much distant theoreticians talk of justice as they forcibly unsort people, and however safe the occupational advantages of intellectuals remain from governmental power."[19] Drawing on his own expertise in intellectual history, Sowell contrasted the prominence and influence of academics in the United States with their counterparts abroad. "Intellectuals have never been as cohesive in the United States as in smaller, more socially homogeneous countries, and the public has never been as thoroughly awed by them," he wrote. "One symptom of this is the utter failure of socialist movements to take root in the United States, while they are strong in Western Europe."[20] But he warned that America must remain on guard against allowing an intellectual class to curtail our individual freedoms in order to advance its notion of social justice: "Freedom is not simply the right of intellectuals to circulate their merchandise. It is, above all, the right of ordinary people to find elbow room for themselves and a refuge from the rampaging presumptions of their 'betters.'"[21]

Sowell had looked forward to writing *Knowledge and Decisions* since the mid-1970s and knew it would be a challenging project. "I thought there was a lot of stuff that needed to be said and it would not be easy to say it," he told me. "It's not the easiest book to read, and it wasn't the easiest book to write, either. This notion of intellectuals as saviors, we've had it for a long time." He said decentralized decision making is a relatively recent phenomenon. For most of human history, the philosopher-king approach—put power in the hands of the right people with the right set of principles—is what prevailed. "One of the things that strikes me about laissez-faire economics—whether with the physiocrats in France or Adam Smith in England—is that it's really a revolutionary doctrine," he said. "It's saying, no, it's not up to Machiavelli or Plato or anybody in between to be able to impose their superior wisdom on others. Because the systemic actions in a marketplace make their interventions in many cases superfluous and in other cases positively harmful. There's some inkling of this is John Stuart Mill when he says that even if the government has more knowledge than anyone in society, it does not have more knowledge than everyone in society."[22]

KNOWLEDGE AND DECISIONS WAS SOWELL'S SIXTH TITLE (in nine years) but the first one reviewed by the *New York Times*, and the paper would continue to review his books throughout the 1980s and 1990s.* The Gray Lady has long been reliably liberal, so it's not surprising that its review quibbled with the book's defense of free markets. However, it also described Sowell as "probably America's most distinguished black social scientist," which surely infuriated any number of black scholars and civil rights activists

---

* For whatever reason, the paper abruptly stopped reviewing Sowell's books more than twenty years ago. As of this writing, the last review to appear was of his memoir, *A Personal Odyssey* (2000). Since then, Sowell has published eighteen books, including two—*The Housing Boom and Bust* (2009) and *Intellectuals and Society* (2010)—that made the paper's own best-seller list.

still smarting over his previous criticisms of racial preferences, mandatory school busing, and minimum-wage
laws. The review also acknowledged that Sowell and other
conservative thinkers had "developed a potent intellectual
framework for analyzing the social order" and provided
"a much needed corrective to the combination of unreflec-
tive moralism, utopian expectations and intellectual pre-
sumption that has too often shaped public policy" in recent
decades. "The free-market viewpoint that Professor Sowell champions is often contemptuously dismissed by others
as either merely a rationalization for economic privilege
or a simplistic call for turning back the clock to an earlier
age," wrote the reviewer, Marc Plattner. "'Knowledge and
Decisions,' by the power and practical relevance of many
of its arguments, offers convincing proof that such assessments are seriously mistaken."[23]

Sowell was generally pleased with the review, even
if he believed certain criticisms were wide of the mark.
"Marc Plattner, I think, made an honest effort to call it as
he saw it," he said at the time. "I just wish he'd seen it more
as I wrote it."[24]

The book was also well received by fellow economists
in the top echelons of the profession. James Buchanan,
a future Nobel laureate, said that it "invites comparison
with Adam Smith's *Wealth of Nations*" and that Sowell
"seems fully at ease with issues of current economic policy,
with economic history, with legal reasoning, with political
and constitutional process, and with the history of ideas.
He seems to be able to call on a veritable mine of wisdom
and experience as he enlightens the discussion of the topics that he explores in depth."[25] Buchanan was no less un-
reserved in his private correspondence with Sowell. "You

have written a great book, and I do not recall ever having said that to anyone," he wrote to him in a letter. "It should be required reading for every social scientist, philosopher, intellectual and politician. I wish I had written it."[26]

Friedrich Hayek, who received the 1974 Nobel Prize in Economics and whose 1946 essay had been the inspiration for *Knowledge and Decisions*, published his own appraisal in *Reason* magazine. Hayek began the review by recalling that when he first received a copy of the book, he put it aside for a period because he was too busy working on his own book to read it. "Now that I have at last studied Professor Sowell's book, I know that that was a mistake," he wrote. "I would have made more rapid progress with my own if I had postponed returning to it until I had fully digested his." Hayek called the book "an original achievement" that "broadened the application" of his own research and "effectively carried the approach into new fields that I never considered." He also praised Sowell's ability to break down abstract and theoretical arguments in terms that could be readily understood by the average person and not just by specialists. "Although his exposition of economic theory is impeccable and contains many original contributions," Hayek concluded, "the strength of the book, its impressiveness and liveliness, is due to his always having before his eyes the concrete phenomena. Simple and vivid illustrations make us aware of the practical implications of his theoretical insights."

Like Buchanan, Hayek noted the book's broad scope, which he considered a major attribute. In addition to his contributions to economics, Hayek wrote widely on psychology and political philosophy. He believed that "an economist who is only an economist cannot even be a good economist." While "an understanding of the market order is a necessary condition for the understanding of our civilization, one has to possess much knowledge of other aspects of civilization in order to comprehend what the market does." To that end, Hayek judged Sowell the full package and called *Knowledge and Decisions* not only "the best book on economics in many a year," and "essential to understanding current affairs," but also "an important philosophical work."[27]

IN TERMS OF ADVANCING SOWELL'S CAREER, HOWEVER, the most consequential praise of the book came from Milton Friedman, who thought so highly of the work that he brought it to the attention of the Hoover Institution on War, Revolution and Peace, where Friedman had landed after retiring from teaching at the University of Chicago in 1977. The institution, which is located on the campus of Stanford University but operates independently, was founded by Stanford alumnus and future US president Herbert Hoover in 1919 for the purpose of creating an archive on the Great War and the Russian Revolution. For many years, its primary focus was foreign affairs, but under the direction of W. Glenn Campbell in the 1970s, the institution expanded its scope. Today, its library of documents on political and social movements in the twentieth century is one of the largest private archives in the United States.

Over time, some of the nation's leading scholars became affiliated with Hoover. They included the Nobel Prize–winning economists George Stigler, Gary Becker, and Kenneth Arrow; historians Robert Conquest, Peter Duignan, and Lewis Gann; the political scientist Seymour

Martin Lipset; the physicist Edward Teller; and the philosopher Sidney Hook. By the end of the 1970s, Sowell was ready for a change and poised to join them. "Although my career was going along well enough, in terms of academic recognition and invitations to give talks and write papers, teaching at UCLA was becoming less and less satisfying," he later wrote.[28] Even the job security of tenure wasn't enough to compensate for the unending administrative meddling, the campus politics, and the overall leftward shift of academia since the 1960s. On the strength of *Knowledge and Decisions*, Hoover made Sowell an offer that was too good to pass up: a Senior Fellow position with no teaching requirements, no hours, and no duties, which would allow him to devote all of his time to research and writing on any subjects of his choosing. He described Hoover as "not only a refuge for scholars who refused to march in ideological lockstep with the fashions of the time, it was a refuge for ideas that were largely banished from academia and the media, but which could not be obliterated so long as they had a base from which inconvenient facts and analyses could be developed and published in books, articles, monographs and op-ed columns."[29]

For Sowell, Hoover was heaven on earth, and he immediately became one of its most prominent and productive scholars. From time to time, Stanford and other schools would try to lure him back into teaching, but he declined their entreaties, just as he would decline offers to fill various political posts. Instead, the 1980s saw Sowell giving more speeches, doing more interviews on radio and television, offering testimony before Congress, and writing a syndicated newspaper column. He also hosted a well-publicized conference called "Black Alternatives" to promote viewpoints that differed from those of traditional civil rights organizations such as the NAACP. And all the while, the books kept coming at a killing pace. Between 1981 and 1985, Sowell published five new works, most of which focused on race and ethnicity. These books stressed the importance of human capital—skills, behaviors, values—in determining a group's economic success. They expanded on an analysis he had first offered in *Race and Economics* back in 1975, and which would culminate with the publication of *Race and Culture* in 1994.

John Raisian, who headed Hoover from 1989 to 2015, and who happens to have been a student of Sowell's at UCLA in the 1970s, explained what Sowell has meant to Hoover. "Honestly, people here viewed him as big-time," he told me. "He was incredibly productive. He was incredibly successful in terms of his [book sales], far above any of our other people by and large. So, he was an anchor. And he was an ideal fit for Hoover because Hoover is trying to educate people about ideology and the pros and cons, and he was just a mastermind at that with his writings."[30]

Sowell's 1981 book *Ethnic America*, a study of the nation's largest racial and ethnic groups, drew far more media attention than any of his previous books, helping to raise his profile as a public intellectual. It was reviewed in the *Wall Street Journal*, the *Washington Post*, *Time*, and *Newsweek* and was on the front page of the *New York Times* book review section. In an appearance on the public affairs program *Tony Brown's Journal* to promote a follow-up to *Ethnic America*, *The Economics and Politics of Race* (1983), Sowell explained how cultural traits tend to follow a group wherever it goes and have far more bearing on economic advancement than how the group is treated by society at large. In this sense, he argued, we are not products of our environment so much as products of our culture, which encompasses more than our immediate surroundings. Thus, you find "the same group having the same characteristics in country after country," he said. The "Germans produced the first pianos in Australia. They created the piano industry in the United States. They built the first pianos in England. They built the first pianos in Russia. You look at the Chinese. What they major in in Malaysia in college is what they major in in the United States in college. . . . So the notion that the group is a creature of society—that society has shaped the group—just will not stand up to the facts."[31]

Sowell's popular books and media appearances during this period also brought him to the attention of a new generation of black thinkers. Gerald Early, a professor of English and black studies at Washington University in St. Louis, told me that *Ethnic America* was his introduction to Sowell and that the book made quite an impression in the early 1980s among his peers. "A lot of people read it and talked about it," he said. "The thing about Sowell that made him really different was not only that he was a conservative but that he was an economist. A lot of the social science debate from the black side of it—from the black folks who I knew in social science circles—was mostly being dominated by people who were in sociology."

Early said that even people who ultimately disagreed with Sowell could appreciate a perspective from a different discipline. "You had this set of black intellectuals who had published and who had dominated and had created a kind of orthodoxy about this from the liberal side," he said, citing mid-twentieth-century figures like E. Franklin Frazier and Kenneth Clark. "On top of this, you've got the wave of people coming into the academy through black studies programs who were definitely advocating something even [further] left. Sowell was something new because he was an economist, and he was going against the orthodoxy of the moment." Early said that the clarity of Sowell's prose added to his appeal:

> You think, "I've got to put the armor on and fight through these pages," but he's a very clear writer. He was enjoyable to read. I knew lots of black people who weren't academics and who had heard about him and were reading his stuff because it was accessible. . . . I was impressed because Sowell really had a certain kind of mastery to do the kind of stuff he was doing. He had some kind of mastery beyond economics. He had some kind of mastery of sociology. He had some kind of mastery of history. He had some kind of mastery of other fields to do the kind of comprehensive stuff he was doing. Whether you agree totally with his ideas or not, it was impressive what he was doing. Who knew an economist could write that stuff?[32]

Sowell was also solidifying his reputation as a formidable debater around this time. He would fact-check journalists on the spot and tussle with critics when he thought that he or his work was being misrepresented. In 1981 he appeared on *Meet the Press*, where he faced questions from the moderator, Bill Monroe, as well as from a panel of antagonistic reporters, including Marvin Kalb, who would later become dean of Columbia University's school of journalism. When one of the reporters prefaced a question by stating that "blacks have made more progress in the last seventeen years than at any other time in history, progress that came about largely as a result of the government social programs during that period, among them affirmative action," Sowell shot back, "I would disagree entirely with you on your facts." He added, "As I've looked at affirmative action, I do not see blacks or Hispanics rising relative to the general population under affirmative action. I think there are a lot of assertions and foregone conclusions that are stated over and over again, but repetition is not a substitute for facts."

Asked to explain the difference between his approach to addressing racial inequality and that of traditional civil rights organizations, Sowell responded, "I have a lot more confidence in what black people can do, if given the opportunity, than some of the other people seem to have. They seem to think that black people must either be led by the hand or else be handed something directly by government. I think that once the opportunities are there, blacks have certainly made the most of such small opportunities as have been available historically, and I see no reason why we wouldn't continue to make use of wider opportunities."

When a panelist stated that "history has shown us that when government failed to take on those responsibilities of providing for upward black mobility and equality and justice, no one did," Sowell took him to task. "The government has been quite active in suppressing the advancement of blacks in the United States as well as in some other countries," he explained. "The great achievement of the civil rights organizations has been getting the government off the backs of blacks, notably in the South with the Jim Crow laws. . . . Where they tried to get government to play a positive role, so-called, that's where they've not only failed but where they've had counterproductive results."[33]

After the program aired, he received a letter from the moderator, Bill Monroe, who thanked him for appearing as a guest. "The panelists, including myself, seemed a little flat-footed," Monroe wrote. "But even if it wasn't as good as it could have been, it had plenty of electricity. Our letters made that clear. About 60 percent of them expressed enthusiastic receptivity to you and what you had to say. (That is a much larger-than-normal favorable proportion.) About 20 percent were outraged by your attitude that blacks don't need government help. And about 20 percent felt that the panel of reporters, Marvin in particular but all of us in general, were outmatched intellectually. . . ."[34]

In 1980, public television aired *Free to Choose*, a ten-episode series of programs hosted by Milton Friedman on the virtues of the free market. In a segment about the welfare state's impact on the underclass, several liberal guests argued that the bigger problem was capitalism itself, which they said necessitates governmental intervention because the free-market system leaves so many people mired in poverty. When it was Sowell's turn to respond, he said the problem was less about the shortcomings of capitalism and more about the perverse incentives that government largess created. He argued that poor people, like other people, weigh costs and benefits when making decisions. And if the government chose to subsidize poverty, it followed that the ranks of the poor would increase. "What the welfare system and other kinds of government programs are doing is paying people to fail. Insofar as they fail, they receive the money. Insofar as they succeed, even to a moderate extent, the money is taken away," he said.

"This is even extended into the school system where they will give money to schools with low scores. Insofar as the school improves its education, the money is taken away. So that you are subsidizing people to fail in their own private lives and become more dependent upon the handouts."[35]

Sowell broadened his attack on the efficacy of government programs for the poor in a 1981 appearance on William F. Buckley's *Firing Line*, saying, "I haven't been able to find a single country in the world where the policies being advocated for blacks in the United States have lifted any people out of poverty." He also took on the argument that sexism explained the gender gap in earnings. "Assertions have been made, not only without any evidence being offered but without anyone even asking for evidence, as if these are self-evident truths that have been brought down from the mountainside," he said. People "say that women make X percent of the income of men without bothering to find out what percentage of those women are working part time, what percentage of those women are reentering the labor force after having children, etc., rather than saying, let us compare women who chose to stay in the labor force continuously since high school on into their thirties, let's say, compared to men who did, and see how do they compare. And there, these great differences tend to disappear. In some cases, the women make more."[36] Later in the same program, during a debate with the lawyer and prominent feminist Harriet Pilpel, the following exchange occurred:

PILPEL: Would it be your feeling that if all the affirmative action programs were discontinued, women and minorities would go ahead much faster than they have under the affirmative action programs?

SOWELL: Yes. It's not my opinion. The data indicate that, for example, the Puerto Ricans had a higher percentage of the national average income before quotas than after. So did Mexican Americans. Blacks had about the same.

PILPEL: Well, [affirmative action] certainly has been a revolution insofar as women's participation in the labor force.

SOWELL: Not really.

PILPEL: I know that of my own knowledge.

SOWELL: No, you don't know it of your own knowledge because I've looked at the same thing. And in the past, you found women overrepresented in many professional occupations, much more so than today. And you find a decline [among women] in those occupations [that is] much more highly correlated with a lower age of marriage for college women and with more childbearing. And as those two things—those two demographic factors—have changed, women have also changed in their representation.[37]

Sowell was no less aggressive when defending himself in print. He released *Markets and Minorities*, a short book on the economic effects of racial discrimination, the same year that *Ethnic America* was published. The *New York Review of Books* ran a lengthy and highly critical review of both volumes by the sociologist Christopher Jencks. Afterward, the editors offered Sowell an opportunity to reply, but he was headed on vacation at the time and initially didn't want to be bothered. "I had been working really hard and I was preparing to go to Yosemite," Sowell told me. "Then someone said to me, 'If you don't answer, they will say that you can't answer.' So, I sat down and wrote my response and pretty much tore him apart."[38]

Sowell began the detailed and highly entertaining rejoinder by citing instance after instance of Jencks clearly putting words in his mouth. He then quoted passages from the books that directly refuted Jencks's claims. According to Jencks, Sowell had argued that discrimination "tends to disappear once markets become competitive," and that "current discrimination in the marketplace has no effect on black earnings." In fact, *Markets and Minorities* said that the "competitiveness of the market puts a price on discrimination, thereby reducing but not necessarily eliminating it." And a reader will search *Ethnic America* in vain for claims that discrimination doesn't exist or has no impact on black incomes. In the book, Sowell had written, "The point here is not to definitively solve the question as to how much of intergroup differences in income, social acceptance, etc., have been due to the behavior and attitudes of particular ethnic groups and how much to the behavior and attitudes of the larger society. The point is that this is a complex question, not a simple axiom."[39] The question is not whether people are discriminated against. The question is to what extent discrimination can explain differences in outcomes. The book's thesis is that different groups brought different cultures to the United States, and that those internal cultures played a bigger role in how these groups fared than did the way they were treated by outsiders. Sowell wasn't saying that discrimination was irrelevant. He was saying that discrimination alone was an insufficient explanation of social inequality.

The Jencks review was an early example of the various lines of attack that would be used against Sowell for the balance of his career. More importantly, it illustrated a favored *method* of attack. Detractors often preferred to respond to what he was supposedly "suggesting" or "implying." They speculated about what he "really" meant or was saying "in effect." This allowed them to distort Sowell's positions and then reply to the distortion instead of addressing what he'd actually said. As Sowell has put it, "People often say that I'm denying that there's racism. On the contrary, racism exists everywhere around the world, down through history. That's one of the reasons it's hard to use it as an empirical explanation for anything. In the United States, for example, Puerto Ricans have lower incomes than blacks. I don't know of anyone who believes Puerto Ricans encounter more discrimination than blacks. Obviously, there must be something else involved besides discrimination."[40]

In Jencks's case, it's not even clear that he read the books under review in their entirety. His essay, which ran some twelve thousand words, made no reference to anything past the first chapter of *Ethnic America*. Indeed, he went beyond mere distortion and simply made stuff up, writing at one point that "Sowell argues for patience." Sowell noted in his response that "I don't even discuss any such thing in either book," and added, "But in the first book I wrote on the subject [*Race and Economics*], I said at the outset: 'History . . . gives little support to the view that time automatically erodes racial aversions, fears, and animosities, or even tames the overt behavior on such feelings.'" Nor would time change the behavior of Sowell's critics, who would continue to willfully twist, oversimplify, and otherwise mischaracterize his views for decades to come. The *New York Review of Books* gave Jencks the last word in the exchange. "Let me begin with an apology," he wrote. "I should not have said that Professor Sowell 'argues for patience.' He doesn't."[41]

6

SOWELL'S VISIONS

"This guy, he's our Hayek!"

WHEN I CONTACTED STEVEN PINKER TO DISCUSS SOWELL'S oeuvre and his legacy as a public intellectual, he mentioned the *New York Review of Books* article from the early 1980s and said it was how he first came across Sowell's name. Little did he know at the time that one day the two men would become good friends. Pinker, an evolutionary psychologist at Harvard, is best known for his popular writings on science and human nature. But his early research focused on language development, and specifically, on how children learn to speak, which is how he came to know Sowell a quarter-century ago.

In 1993, Sowell wrote an unusually personal column about his son, John, who had just graduated from college. The column recounted how John had been mislabeled by some people as a young child because he hadn't started speaking until he was almost four years old. He was a normal kid in other respects—playful, curious, mischievous—and not talking didn't seem to bother him in the least. But it caused his parents a great deal of anxiety, especially because no one could really explain to them what was wrong. Teachers and neighbors and day care center employees thought John might have intellectual disabilities, but specialists found no such indications. It was clear that the little boy understood what was said to him and could follow directions. If anything, tests showed that he was unusually bright and had an excellent memory.

"None of the professionals I consulted had any constructive suggestions, and trying to teach him to talk got nowhere," Sowell wrote. Eventually, John began speaking on his own when he was three months shy of his fourth birthday. "Years later, I learned that there is a whole class of boys who have exactly the same pattern of development as my son. It is an inborn pattern and usually includes special ability in math, music, and memory." Sowell presented the experience as a cautionary tale for other parents, whom he urged to be "on guard" against having their children incorrectly labeled and possibly funneled into special education programs where they may not belong and from which they may never emerge. John turned out to be an especially gifted math student and went on to earn his college degree in computer science.[1]

After the column was published, Sowell was deluged with letters from other parents of children with delayed speech and ultimately decided to write a book about the subject. That's when he reached out to Steven Pinker. "Since one of my specialties is language development in children, he sent me the column and asked if I, myself, studied the syndrome or knew of people who did," Pinker told me. Sowell's book on the subject, *Late-Talking Children*, appeared in 1997, and a follow-up, *The Einstein Syndrome: Bright Children Who Talk Late*, was published four years later. Sowell and Pinker soon found that they shared other interests besides speech pathology, including photography, and several photo safaris together ensued. During one of Pinker's visits to the Bay Area, where Sowell lives, the two camera bugs rented a helicopter and took aerial shots of San Francisco. Pinker also learned that the two of them shared an intellectual interest in theories of human nature and that Sowell had written widely on the subject. Sowell had turned to the topic in the mid-1980s after spending the first part of the decade writing mostly about race and ethnicity.

"After meeting him to talk about late-talking children, I was intrigued enough to start reading some of his books," said Pinker. Many people know of Sowell primarily through his writings on culture and race, but his books on intellectual history and social theory are what initially drew Pinker's attention. He started with *A Conflict of Visions* (1987) and then read *The Vision of the Anointed* (1995) and *Knowledge and Decisions*. Pinker was at work on his own book about human nature, *The Blank Slate*, which would eventually be published in 2002, and Sowell's earlier writings proved to be a valuable resource. "It's pretty conventional wisdom that left-wing and right-wing ideologies hinge on different conceptions of human nature. I wanted to explore that connection, and none has done it better than Tom did," he said. "As a general roadmap to political ideology and how they connect to theories of human nature, I thought [the books] were profound and beautifully documented and, for me, extremely helpful. One of the chapters in *The Blank Slate*, the one called 'Politics,' was based in part on his analysis."[2]

Among his dozens of books, Sowell often refers to *A Conflict of Visions* as his favorite. "It's more mine than anything else," he told C-SPAN in a 1990 interview. "In other words, it doesn't build upon any theory that anyone else has, or anything that's already out there in the literature. It's an attempt to explain why people reach different ideological positions from one another. Why two people similarly well informed and similarly well meaning will reach opposite conclusions, not just on a given issue but on a whole range of issues." Twenty-five years later, the book was still his favorite. "It does something that I don't know any other book does. It tries to show implied assumptions behind conflicting views," he told me. "It also shows that these views are not random. There's a whole set of views that go together even though the topics have no internal connection: Military spending and environmentalism. Monetary policy and drug laws. Rent control and whatever. This implies that there's some set of assumptions in there that ties them together, and I try to show what the assumptions are."[3] In reality, the book may be more than that. If Stephen Hawking's *A Brief History of Time* brought nonphysicists closer to understanding a unified theory of how the universe operates, and Richard Dawkins's *The Selfish Gene* did the same for the Darwinian explanation of how creatures evolve, Sowell's *A Conflict of Visions* does something similar regarding how people think about politics and public policy.

THE BOOK IS THE FIRST IN AN INFORMAL TRILOGY—*THE Vision of the Anointed* and *The Quest for Cosmic Justice* (1999) are the other two—published over a thirteen-year span, and it harks back to his earlier writings on the history of ideas. It is Sowell's attempt to lay out a methodology for explaining what drives our ideological disputes about the nature of reason, freedom, equality, justice, and power. He posits that our pitched debates, which span not only centuries but continents, result mainly from two conflicting conceptions of society and how the world works. The contrasting "visions," as he uses the term, refer to the implicit assumptions that guide a person's thinking. They're hunches or gut instincts—what we sense or feel about a matter even sometimes before we know enough to have an informed opinion. On one side you have the "constrained" or "tragic" vision, which sees mankind as hopelessly flawed. When the libertarian legal scholar Richard Epstein writes that the "study of human institutions is always a search for the most tolerable imperfections," he's expressing a constrained vision of the world that dates back hundreds of years.[4] It's a view encapsulated in Immanuel Kant's famous declaration that "from the crooked timber of humanity no truly straight thing can ever be made," and in Edmund Burke's assertion that we "cannot change the nature of things and of men but must act upon them the best we can."

Those with a tragic view tend to see limits to human betterment. Ridding the world of war or crime or prejudice, however desirable, is unrealistic. Therefore, the focus ought to be on setting up institutions and processes—military defenses, the rule of law, free and fair elections—that help us deal with these problems while understanding that we are unlikely to ever eradicate them:

> In the tragic vision, individual suffering and social evils are inherent in the innate deficiencies of all human beings, whether these deficiencies are in knowledge,

wisdom, morality, or courage. Moreover, the available resources are always inadequate to fulfill all the desires of all the people. Thus there are no "solutions" in the tragic vision, but only trade-offs that still leave many desires unfulfilled and much unhappiness in the world. What is needed in this vision is a prudent sense of how to make the best trade-offs from the limited options available, and a realization that "unmet needs" will necessarily remain—that attempting to fully meet those needs seriatim [one after another] only deprives other people of other things, so that a society pursuing such a policy is like a dog chasing its own tail. Given this vision, particular solutions to particular problems are far less important than having and maintaining the right processes for making trade-offs and correcting inevitable mistakes. To those with the tragic vision, the integrity of processes is crucial—much more so than particular causes.[5]

The opposite of the constrained vision is an "unconstrained" or "utopian" view of the human condition, which rejects the idea of inherent limits on what can be achieved. Mankind is viewed as essentially perfectible in the sense that, through reason and willpower, we can move closer and closer to perfection even if we never reach it. Hence, trade-offs are unnecessary. Social problems can be not merely managed but solved. Ingenuity will overcome scarcity, and nothing is unattainable for all who want it. When Senator Robert F. Kennedy said, "Some men see things as they are and say, why; I dream things that never were and say, why not," he was expressing the unconstrained vision. So was playwright and social critic George Bernard Shaw, when he wrote that human suffering "is neither incurable nor even very hard to cure when you have diagnosed it scientifically."[6]

As with the tragic vision, the ideological origins of the utopian view go back hundreds of years. When the philosopher Jean-Jacques Rousseau wrote in *The Social Contract* (1762) that man "is born free" but "is everywhere in chains," and that "men are not natural enemies," he was expressing a utopian view that our problems stem not from our flawed nature but rather from the institutions that we have constructed. Sowell traces today's debates about "social justice" back at least as far as the British journalist and political philosopher William Godwin's treatise *Enquiry Concerning Political Justice* (1793). In a social analysis that still holds sway today among those with an unconstrained vision, Godwin said that "our debt to our fellow men" includes "all the efforts we could make for their welfare, and all the relief we could supply to their necessities."[7] He wrote, "Not a talent do we possess, not a moment of time, not a shilling of property . . . which we are not obligated to pay into the general bank of common advantage." We have no "right, as it has been phrased, to do what we will with our own," according to Godwin. "We have in reality nothing that is strictly speaking our own."[8]

Earl Warren, the chief justice of the United States from 1954 to 1969, was known for interrupting lawyers who were arguing before the Supreme Court to ask, "But is it *right*? Is it *good*?" His approach can be contrasted with that of Justice Oliver Wendell Holmes, who served on the Supreme Court from 1902 to 1932 and expressed a far more constrained view of jurisprudence. Holmes said that his primary role as a judge was to "apply the law" and "to see that the game is played according to the rules whether I like them or not." The philosophers Adam Smith (1723–1790) and John Rawls (1921–2002) both wrote about justice but had very different conceptions of it. "To Smith, it was essential for the very existence and survival of any society that there be some predictable order, with some degree of moral principle, so that people could pursue their lives with their minds at peace, not destroy each other and the whole social order with unremitting strife over the distribution of financial or other benefits," wrote Sowell. "To Rawls, in any society that is advanced beyond a certain minimum of physical requirements, more justice was categorically more important than more of any other benefit—more important than additional material progress, artistic achievement, or personal or national safety." In Smith's constrained view, "a certain measure of justice was a prerequisite for social survival but, beyond that point, justice was simply one among many social and individual benefits to be weighed against one another." But in Rawls's unconstrained view, "justice remained the over-riding benefit in any society that could be considered civilized."[9]

A CONFLICT OF VISIONS DOES NOT SIMPLY POINT OUT semantic differences among noteworthy intellectuals down through the ages. It explains why people who attend anti-police rallies are also likely to support higher taxes on the wealthy and universal health care, and how those positions can be traced to a utopian view of the human condition outlined by men who were born before the United States even existed. It explains why people who oppose judicial activism are likely to support free-market economic policies, and to do so under a framework of thinking laid out centuries ago by the likes of Edmund Burke and Adam Smith, whose writings they've probably never even read. The eighteenth century's two most significant political revolutions occurred in France and America, and Sowell uses them to illustrate how these differing visions helped shaped those events and thus the course of history:

> Where [the French statesman] Robespierre looked forward to the end of revolutionary bloodshed, "when all people will have become equally devoted to their country and its laws," Alexander Hamilton in *The Federalist Papers* regarded the idea of individual actions "unbiased by considerations not connected with the public good" as a prospect "more ardently to be wished than seriously to be expected." Robespierre sought a solution, Hamilton a trade-off.
>
> The Constitution of the United States, with its elaborate checks and balances, clearly reflected the view that no one was ever to be completely trusted with power. This was in sharp contrast to the French Revolution, which gave sweeping powers, including the power of life and death, to those who spoke in the name of "the people," expressing the Rousseauean "general will." Even when bitterly disappointed with particular leaders, who were then deposed and executed, believers in this vision did not substantially change their political systems or beliefs, viewing the evil as localized in individuals who had betrayed the revolution. . . . To the Federalists, the evil was inherent in man, and institutions were simply ways of trying to cope with it.[10]

In his two related works, *The Vision of the Anointed* and *The Quest for Cosmic Justice*, Sowell focuses on the merits and consequences of these visions, and both books are more polemical as a result. In *A Conflict of Visions*, he doesn't try to hide his own tragic view, but the objective is to describe the two visions as clearly as possible rather than to make a case for one or the other. And that descriptive analysis includes parsing the vocabulary that people have used over time to articulate their points of view:

> Words and concepts which revolve around intention—"sincerity," "commitment," "dedication"—have been central to discussions within the framework of the unconstrained vision for centuries, and the policies sought by this vision have often been described in terms of their intended goals: "Liberty, equality, fraternity," "ending the exploitation of man by man," or "social justice," for example. But in the constrained vision, where man's ability to directly consummate his intentions is very limited, intentions mean far less. Burke referred to "the Beneficial effects of human faults" and to "the ill consequences attending the most undoubted Virtues." Adam Smith's entire economic doctrine of laissez-faire implicitly assumed the same lack of correspondence between intention and effect . . .
>
> In the constrained vision, social processes are described not in terms of intentions or ultimate goals, but in terms of the systemic characteristics deemed necessary to contribute to those goals—"property rights," "free enterprise," or "strict construction" of the Constitution, for example. It is not merely

that there are different goals in the two visions but, more fundamentally, that the goals relate to different things. The unconstrained vision speaks directly in terms of desired results, the constrained vision in terms of process characteristics considered conducive to desired results, but not directly or without many unhappy side effects, which are accepted as part of a trade-off.[11]

Sowell hasn't merely thought through the arguments, he's also thought through the assumptions that underpin the arguments, said Peter Boettke, a professor of economics and philosophy at George Mason University who specializes in the history of economic thought. "I think that the *Conflict of Visions* book is the core idea. That constrained versus unconstrained view of man describes everything about what he's up to," he said. "It's a difference in recognizing that we face constraints, and that when we face constraints we face trade-offs. And it's all about negotiating the trade-offs and what institutions we need in order to negotiate trade-offs. Versus the people who think we don't have to make trade-offs."

Boettke cited Sowell's remark that the first rule of economics is scarcity—there's never enough of anything to placate all those who want it—and the first rule of politics is to ignore the first rule of economics. "Sowell's quip is as relevant today as it's ever been," he said. "The Green New Deal, social justice. This is the problem he identifies in *The Quest for Cosmic Justice* and the problem we still all face." In a sense, Boettke noted, Sowell and his critics are talking past one another. "If you take the unconstrained view, logic and evidence is not going to be your determining factor. What's going to be your determining factor is an aesthetic," he said:

> You think about the apocalyptic theorists today and yesterday. What they have in common is what they spend all their time doing, which is painting an aesthetic for us of the world—the ugly reality of today versus the promise of this world of the future in which there are no trade-offs. So, when Sowell responds to that by forcing them to think about trade-offs and logic and evidence, that to them is unpersuasive because what matters is that the aesthetic is beautiful, and that's their cosmic justice.[12]

BOETTKE, WHO STUDIED UNDER THE NOBEL PRIZE–winning economist James Buchanan, said that these are writings of Sowell that will endure: "My teacher Jim Buchanan used to say, 'Do you want to be read today, in ten years or in a hundred years?' I think we'll still be reading Sowell a hundred years from now."[13]

Of course, centuries of social theory cannot be neatly reduced to two camps, and Sowell doesn't pretend otherwise. Nor does he argue that "Democrat" and "Republican," or "liberal" and "conservative," are perfect substitutes for "utopian" and "tragic," or "unconstrained" and "constrained." In fact, he cautions against doing that, stressing "the pitfalls of mechanically translating unconstrained and constrained visions into the political left and right."[14] The writings of philosophers such as John Stuart Mill and Karl Marx are hybrids of the two visions. Thomas Jefferson was an early supporter of the French Revolution but ultimately backed the separation of powers enshrined in the US Constitution.

"Not every ideological struggle fits [Sowell's] scheme," wrote Stephen Pinker in *The Blank Slate*. "But as we say in social science, he has identified a factor that can account for a large proportion of the variance." Pinker also underscored the ongoing relevance of Sowell's analysis. "Some of today's battles between right and left fall directly out of these different philosophies," he observed, citing debates over taxes, trade, and racial inequality. "Other battles follow in a less obvious way from the opposing visions of human potential. The Tragic Vision stresses fiduciary duties, even when the person executing them cannot see their immediate value, because they allow imperfect beings who cannot be sure of their virtue or foresight to participate in a tested system. The Utopian Vision stresses social responsibility, where people hold their actions to a higher ethical standard."[15]

Pinker is more liberal than Sowell politically, but he told me that reading *A Conflict of Visions*, *The Vision of the Anointed*, *The Quest for Cosmic Justice*, and other Sowell works gave him a deeper and more useful understanding of the conservative thought process. "For me, it was something of a revelation," he said. "Spending my adult life in the kind of liberal cocoon of Cambridge, Massachusetts, I had never really seen a careful exposition of a number of views associated with the right and often, I think, misunderstood and caricatured by the left." Pinker said he was "never tremendously political in the first place," but he thought he "became more politically eclectic" after reading Sowell. In particular, he "became more sympathetic to the rationale behind market economies." Like other close observers of Sowell's work on the history of ideas, Pinker believes it's what best distinguishes him as an intellectual, even if his writings on contemporary racial and political topics have drawn more attention.

"The columns, they spread his ideas to a certain faction of fans, but they may have cut him off from the intellectual mainstream by branding him as an ideologue as opposed to a wide-ranging scholar, which I think is what he truly is," said Pinker. "I hope that the political polemicist inside of him does not overshadow the thinker, because, I mean, I've been a professor for thirty-seven years. I've spent my life at Harvard, Stanford, MIT. And I would certainly count Tom as one of the most brilliant people I've come across and one of the deepest thinkers."[16]

EACH BOOK IN SOWELL'S INFORMAL TRILOGY ON THE HIStory of ideas can stand alone, but what they represent collectively is an extensive discourse on methods of thinking about the nature of man. They are his stab at explaining why things are the way they are, and why our discussions of public policy have veered in certain directions for the past two hundred years. What is more, these works are essential guides to where Sowell is coming from, whether the topic is crime control, education policy, international affairs, racial preferences, antitrust law, or some other contemporary subject. They provide the deepest understanding of his approach to processing the world around him.

Sowell's critique of nation-building, for example, is rooted in a belief that the whole concept "is a fundamental misconception. Nations may grow and evolve but cannot be built."[17] His defense of the traditional family, and his criticisms of the welfare-state expansions that have undermined it, stem from an understanding that families—not outside third parties, not government, not "society"—have been essential decision-making units down through history and are best positioned to socialize the next generation. His critique of the civil rights leadership's shift in the post-1960s era away from a focus on equal opportunity and toward a focus on equal results is, at its root, a critique of embracing an unconstrained vision of what is even possible. As Sowell has observed, "If blacks and whites in the United States were the same, they would be the only two groups on the planet who are the same."[18] Likewise, his criticism of the push for slavery reparations flows from his rejection of a utopian view of fairness and justice that dates from William Godwin in the eighteenth century to John Rawls in the twentieth century to Ta-Nehisi Coates in the twenty-first. Even Sowell's analysis of the role of an intellectual like himself is filtered through this template. Within the constrained vision, he writes, "a scholar's moral duty is to faithfully promote the intellectual process among his students and his readers, not lead them to specific conclusions he sincerely believes to be best for society."[19]

Donald Horowitz, a Duke University political scientist and legal scholar, told me that it is Sowell's "methodological critique of policy reasoning" that most impresses him. "He's very good at skepticism and the steps necessary to be an intelligent skeptic," he noted, and then offered an example from a discussion on gun control in *The Thomas Sowell Reader*, where, Horowitz said, Sowell "shows how inept are the comparisons between the United States and the United Kingdom." The standard argument, as Horowitz summarized it, is that "the UK has very few guns and a lot of gun control and very few murders, [while] the United States has a lot of guns, relatively limited gun control, and many murders. Therefore, that's what's responsible for it. But then he goes back and shows that even when the UK had very little gun control and many more guns, there were also very few murders there." Horowitz added, "The fallacy in causal reasoning is brilliantly exposed, I think, in those pieces."[20]

Christopher DeMuth, a former head of the American Enterprise Institute think tank who first met Sowell more than thirty years ago, also admires his seemingly effortless ability to make mincemeat of sloppy thinking. "He's living this life of the mind that has been there as long as I've known him," said DeMuth. "Any subject that comes up, he seems to have a fully formed view of the universe and how it fits into this architecture of thinking. And that is the most distinctive thing about him."

DeMuth agrees that Sowell's most important contributions are his writings on intellectual history and ideas. "Among his books, the vision trilogy influenced my own thinking the most, but the first book I read by him was *Knowledge and Decisions*, and it made a huge impression on me," he said. "When I read that, I thought, 'This guy, he's our Hayek.'" Like Pinker, however, DeMuth suspects that Sowell has been pigeonholed in the intellectual world for his writings on cultural issues. "I can remember thinking once that the one black person I know who's really been a victim of racial discrimination may be Tom Sowell," he told me. "If he weren't black, people would realize what a great economist he was. But they put him in this category because he writes about race and he's got all these contrarian views. And people don't realize that there is this immense intellectual corpus that this man has written on a completely different subject. If he were a Jewish white guy at the University of Chicago, he'd be better recognized for what he is, which is one of the greatest living economists."[21]

7

CIVIL RIGHTS AND WRONGS

"When you want to help people, you
tell them the truth. When you want to
help yourself, you tell them what they
want to hear."[1]

JUST MONTHS BEFORE HIS DEATH IN 1962, THE BLACK
sociologist E. Franklin Frazier published an essay titled
"The Failure of the Negro Intellectual." Like Sowell,
Frazier had attended Howard University and the University of Chicago, where he earned his PhD in 1931. His specialty was the black family, with a particular focus on the
effects of urbanization on millions of rural blacks who had
found their way to cities in the early decades of the twentieth century. His pioneering studies in the 1930s and 1940s
were considered authoritative among white and black
scholars alike. The Swedish economist Gunnar Myrdal's
landmark analysis of US race relations, *An American Dilemma*, drew heavily from Frazier's research, as did Daniel
Patrick Moynihan's 1965 government study, *The Negro
Family: The Case for National Action*.

Like Sowell decades later, Frazier earned a reputation as an independent thinker, a stickler for high academic standards who was willing to challenge his peers in the academy as well as in the civil rights establishment. He criticized the NAACP's efforts at the time to get black colleges to offer more graduate degrees, charging that it was not paying enough attention to whether these schools had enough faculty members with the training or ability to administer graduate-level curricula. "Frazier insisted that most black colleges did not have enough high-caliber faculty members to mount a respectable graduate program," wrote William Banks in his book *Black Intellectuals*. "To initiate second-rate graduate programs simply because blacks were not being admitted to white graduate schools was indefensible, he maintained. Instead, schools should continue to concentrate on their undergraduate programs until their faculties were strong enough to offer advanced-degree programs."[2] Frazier's 1957 book, *Black Bourgeoisie*, ruffled even more feathers with its devastating portrait of middle-class blacks as insular, pretentious, and obsessed with protecting their status. The book made Frazier something of a pariah at Howard University, where he was chairman of the sociology department. Some faculty members refused to attend meetings where he was present. Frazier was unfazed. Indeed, his critique of black scholars was an extension of his broader assessment of black elites in general. He doubled down.

Frazier believed that the adoption of American mainstream values, over time, was essential to black upward mobility. His knock on black intellectuals was that they were putting too much faith in integration alone to address the cultural deficits of the black underclass. "As far as I have been able to discover, what Negro intellectuals have had to say concerning integration has been concerned with the superficial aspects of increasing participation of Negroes in the economic and social and political organization of American society," he wrote in an essay. "Practically no attention has been directed to the rather obvious fact that integration involves the interaction of the organized social life of the Negro community with the wider American community."[3] For this to occur, he contended, there would have to be more focus on the internal development of blacks, yet the "American Negro intellectual, seduced by dreams of final assimilation, has never regarded this as his primary task." Integration, by itself, Frazier continued, wouldn't address the more fundamental problem, which was that large numbers of blacks with "little education" and "practically no skills" were "unprepared for employment in an industrial society, and . . . unfit for normal social life." Frazier said that instead of acknowledging this reality and working to address it, many black scholars were "engaged in petty defenses of the Negro's social failures":

> As long as 25 years ago I pointed out that urbanization had changed the entire relationship of Negroes to American society and that comprehensive and fundamental research should be done on Negroes in cities. But those Negroes who have controlled the destiny of Negro intellectuals ignored this and even today no Negro college or university is concerned with this fundamental problem. . . .
>
> The significance of the large proportion of unemployed, impoverished and socially and personally disorganized Negroes in cities for our discussion cannot

be overemphasized. It shows clearly that whereas a relatively large middle class is emerging in our cities, at the same time a large degraded proletariat is also appearing.[4]

Frazier had long guarded against analyzing American blacks in isolation. Any proper assessment of the black experience necessitated a historical approach that would take into account "all the factors, psychological, social, and economic, which determine the character of any group."[5] His own research included studies of race and culture in Brazil and the West Indies, and he lamented that his fellow intellectuals seldom put the history of black Americans in a wider, international context: "They have failed to study the problems of Negro life in America in a manner which would place the fate of the Negro in the broad framework of man's experience in this world."[6]

Sowell did not agree with all of Frazier's conclusions, but he considered him a first-rate scholar—a Chicago school empiricist guided by the facts, even when they led to unpopular or uncomfortable results—and he has frequently highlighted Frazier's work in his own writings. More importantly, in his scholarship in ways large and small, he has attempted to address many of the shortcomings in the literature that Frazier identified. Sowell has stressed the importance of acquiring cultural capital in black advancement, for example. He has warned against prioritizing the racial integration of political and social institutions as a panacea for what ails the black poor. And he has stressed international comparisons in assessing social inequality. These are the themes that Sowell turned to in earnest in the 1980s and 1990s, and it is the work for which he is best known.

SOME OF SOWELL'S ADMIRERS IN THE ACADEMY BELIEVED that he would have been better off professionally by continuing to focus on economics and intellectual history while avoiding racial topics, but Sowell didn't feel he had that luxury. He saw many current approaches to helping blacks as misguided at best, and he felt compelled to say so, come what may. He had become an economist in the first place to better understand the world around him, and he wanted to share what he'd learned with the public and with policy makers, if only to explain the track record of what had been tried in the past. Minimum-wage laws were pricing blacks out of jobs. Racial preferences in college admissions were setting up smart black kids to fail and fomenting resentment among other groups. Opposition to parental choice was keeping low-income blacks trapped in failing public schools. Government aid was increasing dependency. Above all, there was an abiding belief that bigotry alone was a sufficient explanation for why some groups lagged behind others, and that stamping out discrimination ought to be the highest priority.

Sowell had platforms—at Stanford's Hoover Institution, in his columns, in his books, in his access to the media—and he felt a certain scholarly duty to use those platforms to offer alternative perspectives. Unfortunately, the discussion about race was being driven by emotion and political correctness when he thought that the standard—among intellectuals, at least—ought to be evidence and logic. In the Chicago school tradition, Sowell sought to use his training to apply economic reasoning to the real world of ordinary people. Considering the strong liberal bent of the media and the traditional black leadership, if someone with his background and perspective didn't speak out on these touchy topics, how would people learn that there was a different way of addressing the challenges that blacks faced?

In the early 1980s, Sowell had been planning a book on Marxian economics, but as the twentieth anniversary of the 1964 Civil Rights Act approached, he determined that "someone ought to present some of the things . . . [people are] not likely to hear in this discussion."[7] So he put aside the manuscript on Marxism and wrote *Civil Rights: Rhetoric or Reality?*, a book that questioned the assumptions—the utopian vision—of self-appointed black leaders. The civil rights establishment had long operated under the assumption that racial discrimination largely explained statistical disparities in achievement and that, in the absence of bias toward minority groups, we would see more equitable outcomes. Another assumption was that political activity was essential to the economic advancement of a racial or ethnic minority group. In the book, Sowell submitted both assumptions to empirical tests and found them wanting. "Groups with a demonstrable history of being discriminated against have, in many countries and in many periods of history, had higher incomes, better educational performance, and more 'representation' in high-level positions than those doing the discriminating," he wrote.[8] The civil rights vision couldn't explain those outcomes: "That Jews earn far higher incomes than Hispanics in the United

States might be taken as evidence that anti-Hispanic bias is stronger than anti-Semitism—if one followed the logic of the civil rights vision. But this explanation is considerably weakened by the greater prosperity of Jews than Hispanics *in Hispanic countries* throughout Latin America."[9]

Sowell likewise used the experience of various other ethnic minority groups, in America and elsewhere, to push back at the idea that black political clout was a prerequisite for black social and economic upward mobility. Seeking political office became a major focus of black leaders after the passage of the Voting Rights Act of 1965. The theory was that more black elected officials would lead to less social inequality, but that's not what happened. By the early 1980s major US cities with large black populations—Cleveland, Detroit, Chicago, Washington—had elected black mayors. Between 1970 and 2010, the number of black elected officials grew from fewer than 1,500 to more than 10,000 and included Barack Obama, the first black president. Yet even as blacks were increasing their political clout in the 1970s, 1980s, and 1990s, black welfare dependency was rising, as was black crime, black teen unemployment, and births to single black women. None of this surprised Sowell, who had researched the patterns of other groups as well as the history of black American progress before the civil rights leadership's strategic shift in emphasis.

"Among groups that have gone into other countries, begun at the bottom and later rose past the original or majority inhabitants are the Chinese in southeast Asia, the Caribbean and the United States. In all these very different settings, the Chinese have studiously avoided politics," he wrote. Political activity "has played little, if any, role in the often dramatic rises of the Chinese from poverty to affluence."[10] Nor were the Chinese outliers in this regard. "This pattern has likewise been characteristic of the Germans in the United States, Brazil and Australia," Sowell continued. Sometimes the minority group chose to avoid politics. Other times, a group was not given a choice: "Jews were for centuries kept out of political rule in a number of countries, either by law, by custom, or by anti-Semitic feeling in the elite or in the populace. But even where political careers were at least theoretically open to them, as in the United States, Jews only belatedly sought public office, and in the United States were at first wholly subservient to Irish political bosses."[11] He noted the Irish as an example of a group that prioritized politics only to discover that it did not hasten their economic rise in America:

> The Irish have been perhaps the most striking example of political success in an ethnic minority, but their rise from poverty was much *slower* than that of other groups who were nowhere near being their political equals. Irish-run political machines dominated many big city governments in America, beginning in the latter part of the nineteenth century, but the great bulk of the Irish populace remained unskilled laborers and domestic servants into the late nineteenth century. The Irish were fiercely loyal to each other, electing, appointing and promoting their own kind, not only in the political arena but also in the hierarchy of the Catholic Church. This had little effect on the average Irish American, who began to reach economic prosperity in the twentieth century at about the time when

the Irish political machines began to decline and when Irish control of the Catholic Church was increasingly challenged by other groups.[12]

After documenting that "political activity and political success have been neither necessary nor sufficient for economic advancement," he speculated as to why ethnic leaders nevertheless pushed the notion that political clout was decisive, even if it was to the detriment of the groups they claimed to represent. In short, as E. Franklin Frazier had noted decades earlier, it was because these elites had their own agenda. "Groups that have the skills for other things seldom concentrate in politics," wrote Sowell. "Moreover, politics has special disadvantages for ethnic minority groups, however much it may benefit individual ethnic leaders. Public displays of ethnic solidarity and/or chauvinism are the life blood of ethnic politics. Yet chauvinism almost invariably provokes counter-chauvinism."[13] Civil rights organizations wanted to raise money and stay relevant, and black politicians who ran as ethnic leaders wanted to win votes. Which meant they had a vested interest in framing black problems primarily as civil rights problems even when the evidence pointed to other factors.

Sowell has never denied that racism still existed or that it could exacerbate racial disparities. Nor has he posited that blacks should stay out of politics or that the civil rights movement was unnecessary or unhelpful in making America more just. In a private letter, he once wrote that the "historic significance of the civil rights era was that it completed the American Revolution by making it apply to *all* people."[14] He applauded the landmark civil rights bills of the 1960s but cautioned against giving that legislation—and political activity in general—more credit than preexisting black trendlines showed it deserved. "Much has been made of the fact that the numbers of blacks in high-level occupations increased in the years following passage of the Civil Rights Act of 1964," he wrote. "But the number of blacks in professional, technical and other high-level occupations more than doubled in the decade *preceding* the Civil Rights Act of 1964. In other occupations, gains by blacks were greater during the 1940s—when there was practically no civil rights legislation—than during the 1950s. In various skilled trades, the income of blacks relative to whites more than doubled between 1936 and 1959. The trend was already under way."[15]

Sowell obviously was not arguing for a return to Jim Crow. Rather, he was describing what had been accomplished by blacks when they faced widespread legal discrimination and enjoyed next to no political power. He was explaining that people who claimed that the black middle class today is a product of civil rights legislation enacted in the 1960s and affirmative action policies implemented in the 1970s simply didn't have the facts on their side. He was saying that racial discrimination was an insufficient explanation of social inequality, given what blacks had been able to accomplish in American society in an earlier era when racism was legal and far more widespread.

Civil Rights: Rhetoric or Reality? compares the intentions of liberalism with the reality of what has occurred. As in his studies of other phenomena, Sowell evaluated racial progress through a "constrained" and "unconstrained" methodology. What matters most is not the plausibility of a theory but whether the facts and evidence support it. And after taking an empirical approach to analyzing the various strategies advanced by ethnic leaders and left-wing policy makers in the name of helping blacks, Sowell stated plainly what wasn't working and why. He wasn't opposed to civil rights or to civil rights organizations per se. But he was opposed to pursing strategies that had a track record of failure and that might be doing considerable harm to the intended beneficiaries even as they benefited the mainstream black leadership. "Despite much racial progress, there have also been some very fundamental disappointments," he wrote. "Ghettos persist, and in many ways are becoming worse for those trapped in them. School integration has largely been thwarted by the demographic facts of 'white flight.' But even where it has occurred, it has produced neither the education nor the social miracles once expected." The outlook was bleak:

> Job barriers have come down but black teenage unemployment has soared to several times what it was 30 years ago. Many white allies in the early struggles for civil rights have become critics of the later phases, such as affirmative action and busing. A small but growing number of black critics has also appeared.
>
> How and why this all happened is a long and complicated story. In essence, however, two things have happened: (1) the battle for civil rights was won, decisively, two decades ago, and (2) the succeeding years have painfully revealed that blatant denials of civil rights were not the universal explanation of social or racial problems.[16]

Civil Rights: Rhetoric or Reality? is only 140 pages long, but nearly four decades after its publication it continues to punch well above its weight. Even the election of a black president—the culmination of a civil rights strategy in place since the 1960s—did not produce the black advancement that was promised. Under Barack Obama's two terms as president, black-white gaps in income and homeownership widened, and by the time he left office polls showed that race relations had fallen to their lowest point in nearly a quarter-century.[17] Moreover, black leaders and their sympathizers on the progressive left remained as wedded as ever to the notion that past and present racial discrimination was the biggest barrier to black progress. Liberals continued to defend group preferences, even though, as Sowell put it in 1999, these advocates "have yet to explain why something that happened 40 years ago justifies discrimination against some guy who is 39."[18]

Celebrated writers such as Ta-Nehisi Coates have called for slavery reparations to address inequality. Black Lives Matter activists target policing and Confederate statuary. The *New York Times*'s "1619 Project" rewrites US history in a manner that puts the subjugation of blacks at the center of the nation's founding. "For many, 'discrimination' and 'racism' are not partial truths but whole truths, not just things to oppose but explanations to cling to, like a security blanket," Sowell concluded.[19] The rhetoric continues to trump reality. *Civil Rights: Rhetoric or Reality?* "was a painful book to write," he said in a personal letter after the book's publication. "But other Americans have done more painful things than that, or none of us would be here, living in freedom today. My dues were small."[20] He dedicated the book to "E. Franklin Frazier, who put truth above popularity."

THE SEMINAL ECONOMIC ANALYSIS OF RACIAL BIAS IS
Gary Becker's *The Economics of Discrimination* (1957),
which used price theory to measure the extent of racism
in labor markets and challenged the Marxist view that discrimination inevitably benefits the one who discriminates.
Becker was a former professor of Sowell's and another
product of the Chicago school under Milton Friedman.
"When Becker first began his career, no one expected economists to talk about racial issues," Sowell wrote in a column after Becker was awarded the Nobel Prize in 1992.
"Single-handedly, he created a whole new field of economics. After more than three decades, Becker's analysis of
racial discrimination is widely used by other economists."[21]

Becker's book is a highly technical work written for
fellow economists and not the general public, but its central observation is that in a free market, discrimination
imposes costs not only on the person being discriminated
against but also on the person inflicting the discrimination. Theoretically, therefore, market competition can de-
ter discriminatory behavior by putting those who practice
it at a disadvantage against rivals who don't. If a landlord
won't rent to Hispanics, for example, he runs the risk of
leaving apartments vacant for a longer period of time and
losing income. If an employer hires unqualified whites as
a result of prejudice against blacks, his business could become less productive and lose market share to other businesses that hire regardless of race. The competitive market,
in which supply and demand drive decision-making, re-
duces the possibilities for discrimination. To the extent
that government policies interfere with free markets in
ways that make them less competitive—through housing

regulations or minimum-wage laws, for example—the costs of discrimination are reduced. Becker was not arguing that free-market capitalism would eradicate racial bias in employment or housing. In fact, he wrote that "the persistence of such discrimination against blacks shows that competition and free enterprise do not by themselves eliminate the effects of prejudice."[22] Still, his research suggested that the best protection against discrimination is a competitive market that can exact a price on those who choose to exercise their biases.

Becker's application of economic analysis to sociology, history, law, and other fields of study was not always appreciated by sociologists, historians, and legal scholars. But it was an approach that Sowell fully embraced early on in books, such as *Race and Economics* (1975) and *Markets and Minorities* (1980), which examine the economic and social condition of racial and ethnic groups in a historical context. And, like Becker, Sowell took an empirical approach. "Whatever the merits or moral philosophical arguments," he wrote in *Race and Economics*, "cause-and-effect analysis is needed to analyze the scope, magnitude, and variation of discrimination over time, the degree to which various market and nonmarket forces intensify or reduce discrimination, the extent to which various behavior patterns within a minority group advance or retard its economic progress, and to judge the consequences of various possible approaches to dealing with the problem."[23]

Sowell's 1981 best seller, *Ethnic America*, picked up on these themes, but critics objected to his contention that culture played a larger role than discrimination in the fate of various ethnic groups in the United States. In response, he broadened the scope of his analysis to include examples from other parts of the world, as well as examples of the role that politics can play in a minority group's progress. He looked at how Germans had fared in Brazil, at how the Chinese had fared in Indonesia, and at how Jews had fared in Spain. Alas, the same patterns he had documented among ethnic groups in America were seen in other countries. The resulting book was *The Economics and Politics of Race: An International Perspective* (1983).

Multiculturalists in the academy and in the media were trying to have it both ways, he said. On the one hand, they argued that ethnic cultures were unique, which was true. At the same time, they refused to address the economic consequences of those differences, which was intellectually dishonest. "Much of the literature on racial, national and cultural groups attempts to be neutral on group differences," Sowell wrote. "But to ignore the large role that performance differences have played in human history is to ignore or misdiagnose important causal factors at work in that history. Cultures are ultimately ways of accomplishing things, and the differing efficiencies with which they accomplish different things determine the outcomes of very serious economic, political and military endeavors."[24] Taking a multidisciplinary approach to the subject, Sowell also explained how political incentives make it "difficult to correctly diagnose problems in public, and without correct diagnosis, correct prescription is unlikely." He then elaborated on this concept:

> Political approaches to economic problems must be
> (1) emotionally acceptable to those whom leaders

address, and (2) must offer "solutions" that at least plausibly lie within the political domain. Therefore, whatever the real complex of forces at work or the relative weights of various factors, political leaders tend to emphasize—sometimes exclusively—those factors for which a law or policy can be formulated. . . . Factors such as intergroup differences in demographic characteristics, geographical distribution, skill levels or cultural values tend to be ignored, however demonstrably important they may be in a cause-and-effect sense. In short, political "solutions" tend to misconceive the basic issues. . . . [T]hese misconceptions may serve the political leadership well, even if they are counterproductive for the racial or ethnic group in whose name they speak.[25]

It was yet another decades-old analysis of Sowell's that has lost none of its relevance over time. The violent summer protests that followed the death of George Floyd in 2020 were fueled by a narrative that accused police of unjustly targeting blacks with lethal force. It was a narrative driven primarily by viral videos on social media and other anecdotal evidence. The empirical data available, however, showed no evidence of racial bias in police shootings. In fact, the data showed that black and Hispanic suspects were *less* likely than white suspects to be shot at by police. There were also studies that demonstrated a marked *decline* in police shootings overall in recent decades. The disproportionate number of encounters between black suspects and law enforcement was a function of disproportionately high violent-crime rates among blacks, not police bias.[26] Nevertheless, activists, the mainstream media, and many politicians had no incentive to highlight this evidence and rarely did so, even though unfairly vilifying cops in the past had resulted in less effective policing and more violent crime in black communities.[27]

SOWELL'S CRITICS IN THE ACADEMY OFTEN TAKE ISSUE WITH his application of economic thinking to noneconomic disciplines. In a review of *Ethnic America* in a 1982 issue of *The Yale Review*, for example, the historian Nathan Irvin Huggins called the book "problematic, both conceptually and methodologically." Why? "It assumes that ethnic groups in America can be compared, one to another, better to understand why some succeed well and others not at all." Huggins considered such comparisons "vulgar exercises." Sowell's alleged "unqualified faith in the 'market' to reward the most productive and efficient person" also bothered him. "Were his clumsy comparisons merely innocent intellectual parlor games they would be bad enough," wrote Huggins, "but because he is a social scientist of high repute Sowell's work has pernicious influence."

In other words, Huggins was saying that we couldn't have this distinguished scholar applying a different type of analysis to the history of ethnic groups. Sowell needed to stay in his lane, you see, because this wasn't how we historians approached these matters. Blacks were a special case, and comparing them to other groups was "inappropriate" and "simple-minded." Huggins's review was far more focused on refuting Sowell's *way of thinking* about ethnic and racial inequality—how "Sowell's mind works," as the review put it—than it was on refuting the actual facts and evidence and logic presented in the book, which were treated almost as an afterthought.[28]

While some fault Sowell for bridging academic disciplines in his analyses of the civil rights movement, migration, or other topics, there are others who insist that it's one of the best features of his scholarship. William R. Allen, a former chairman of the economics department at UCLA, where Sowell taught in the 1970s, applauded his former colleague's use of empirical analyses outside of economics. "People like [Milton] Friedman and [George] Stigler and Ronald Coase and others at Chicago had a genuine interest in and feel for and sense of empiricism, which was manifested in one way or another," he told me. "But Tom goes much further than they did in bringing in the sociology, the history, the political science, geography and psychology. In fact, the economics, in any pure isolated sense, well, it doesn't disappear, but it's just one element of many. He's about as much a sociologist and historian as he is economist, but he does it very, very well."[29]

In an appreciation of Sowell published by the *Claremont Review of Books* in 2017, the writer Mark Helprin was even more effusive. "There has always been peril in ranging across history and disciplines and thus trespassing upon the turf of various tenured dunces entrapped in the tiny thickets of their own making," he wrote. "Sowell is one of the great trespassers, as a great man must be, unafraid to go wherever his talent for elucidation takes him. And this clarity of vision, a strong light that effortlessly shatters the darkness of cant and purposeful misconstrual, repeatedly brightens his chosen fields of battle to the point of stunning his opponents and delighting all others." The way he wields not only economics, but also "logic, rhetoric, history, geography, demography, anthropology, political philosophy, and even geophysics as his instruments of analysis" is almost preternatural. "That is perhaps the essence of what he does, the melding in one revelation after another of his exceptional talents in a way that surpasses their sum."[30]

8

CULTURE MATTERS

"Each group trails the long shadow of its
own history and culture, which influence
its habits, priorities, and social patterns,
which in turn affect its fate."[1]

IN 1966, IRVING KRISTOL PUBLISHED A LENGTHY ESSAY IN
the *New York Times Magazine* under the headline "The
Negro Today Is Like the Immigrant Yesterday." At the time,
Kristol was editor of a highbrow quarterly, *The Public
Interest*, and a senior book editor at a New York publishing house. In the *Times* article he noted that what he was
reading about blacks seldom reflected the "facts of Negro
life in America" at the time, and pointed out that the same
had been true of literature on immigrant groups in an earlier era. There was a tendency to highlight black "pathology" and ignore or play down clear upward mobility. He
cited data showing a sharp decline in black poverty rates,
improvements in housing, and a rapidly growing black
middle class. "But all this receives little attention from
our writers and sociologists, both of whom are concerned
with the more dramatic, and less innocently bourgeois,

phenomena of Negro life," Kristol wrote. "This is to be expected of the writers; it is less expected of sociologists, and the antibourgeois inclination of so much of current American sociology would itself seem to be an appropriate subject for sociological exploration."

Kristol worried that scholars weren't putting the black experience into the context it deserved. Yes, the move from rural to urban environs had been rocky for blacks, but that same shift had taken a toll on Irish and Italian immigrants, among others, as well. Nor was this a pattern that could only be found in America. The migration of the rural pro-letariat to cities in nineteenth-century England and France had likewise been a difficult one.

"One does wish that those who are professionally concerned with our Negro urban problem, while not los-ing their capacity for indignation or their passion for re-form, could avail themselves of such a longer view," wrote Kristol. "After all, that presumably is what their profes-sional training was for. One could also wish that these same scholars were less convinced a priori of the unique-ness of the Negro's problem and more willing to think in terms of American precedents."[2]

Sowell was an assistant professor of economics at Cornell at the time, and the piece caught his attention. "He had some interesting facts in there," he told me, recalling the article as "one of the first things I saw" that compared the experiences of blacks with those of certain immigrant groups in the United States. But it wasn't until he read Nathan Glazer and Daniel Patrick Moynihan's classic 1963 study of racial and ethnic minorities in New York City, *Beyond the Melting Pot*, that Sowell would become interested in conducting his own comparative analyses of different cultures. "It was really the first book I read about different ethnic groups. There were many different patterns. And more than anything else, each group had its own pattern," he said:

> The left likes to portray a group as sort of a creature of surrounding society. But that's not true. For example, back during the immigrant era, you had neighborhoods on the Lower East Side [of Manhattan] where Jews and Italians arrived at virtually identical times. Lived in the same neighborhoods. Kids sat side by side in the same schools. But totally different outcomes. Now, if you look back at the history of the Jews and the history of the Italians you can see why that would be. In the early nineteenth century, Russian officials report that even the poorest Jews find some way to get some books in their home, even though they're living in a society where over 90 percent of the people are illiterate.
>
> Conversely, in southern Italy, which is where most Italian Americans originated, when they put in compulsory school-attendance laws, there were riots. There were schoolhouses burning down. So now you take these two kids and sit them side by side in a school. If you believe that environment means the immediate surroundings, they're in the same environment. But if you believe environment includes this cultural pattern that goes back centuries before they were born, then no, they're not in the same environment. They don't come into that school building with the same mindset. And they don't get the same results.[3]

Toward the end of 1995, Sowell contacted Jim Michaels, the editor of *Forbes* magazine, where he had published a popular column since 1991. He explained that he was stretched too thin and would have to stop writing regularly for the magazine. He was sixty-five years old at the time and wanted to devote more energy to finishing his trilogy. "My top priority has to be completing a huge manuscript that I began writing in 1982 and which has thus far produced two books—*Race and Culture* and *Migrations and Cultures*—and will produce a third, *Conquests and Cultures*, in a couple years," he told Michaels. "This international cultural history seems to me to be not only the most important thing I can leave behind me, but also one of the most urgently needed things, at a time when the Balkanization and polarization of this country are truly dangerous prospects."[4]*

Sowell circumnavigated the world twice in the 1980s to gather data from a variety of societies he wished to compare. Stops included England, Israel, Greece, India, Hong Kong, Singapore, Australia, and Fiji. This field research would inform not just the trilogy but also Sowell's other international perspectives and histories for the balance of his career. It's evident in any number of subsequent books, including *The Economics and Politics of Race* (1983),

---

* Given that Sowell was expressing worry about the "truly dangerous prospects" of "polarization" in America back in 1995, at a time of relative peace and prosperity in the country predating the controversial election of President George W. Bush, the wars in Afghanistan and Iraq, the Great Recession, the election of President Donald Trump, and the Covid-19 pandemic of 2020, Sowell is either unduly pessimistic by nature or unearthily prescient.

Preferential Policies (1990), *Affirmative Action Around the World* (2004), *Black Rednecks and White Liberals* (2005), and *Wealth, Poverty and Politics* (2015). In these volumes, he intertwines his own observations with those of specialists who have come before him. Influential predecessors and foundational works include Victor Purcell's *The Chinese in Southeast Asia*, Charles Price's *Southern Europeans in Australia*, Ellen Churchill Semple's *Influence of Geographic Environment*, N. J. G. Pounds's *An Historical Geography of Europe*, and Bernard Lewis's studies on the history of the Islamic world. "There would of course be no point standing on the shoulders of giants if we saw only what they saw and simply repeated what they had already said, often quite well," he wrote. "But we can at least look in different directions from the vantage point they give us, and seek answers to other questions with the benefit of the knowledge and insight they provided."[5] Sowell has made a career of looking in "different directions," nowhere more so than in his writings on racial, ethnic, and cultural patterns.

BECAUSE SO MANY SOWELL CRITICS BRING WHAT HE considered to be an unconstrained or utopian perspective to discussions of public policy, strong disagreements are predictable, if not inevitable. Sowell's view was that problems such as discrimination and social inequality were part of the human condition and couldn't definitively be "solved," but only managed to the best of our abilities through processes and institutions that have stood the test of time. Thus, there are no "solutions" in the offing, only trade-offs. "Much of what are called 'social problems' consists of the fact that intellectuals have theories that do not fit the real world," he wrote. "From this they conclude that it is the real world which is wrong and needs changing."[6]

Sowell rejected that unconstrained view. "It should be axiomatic that there is not unlimited time, unlimited resources, or unlimited good will among peoples— anywhere in the world," he said. "If we are serious about wanting to enlarge opportunities and advance those who are less fortunate, then we cannot fritter away the limited means at our disposal in quixotic quests. We must decide whether our top priority is to smite the wicked or to advance the less fortunate, whether we are looking for visions and rhetoric that make us feel good for the moment or whether we are seeking methods with a proven track record of success in advancing whole peoples from poverty to prosperity."[7]

As discussed earlier, Sowell's research undermined the notion that racial and ethnic disparities could be laid to genetics. But he was also skeptical of claims that past hostility or discrimination visited upon minorities by majorities sufficiently explained why some groups trailed others. "One of the strongest arguments against the injustice explanation of intergroup differences is that, in many countries around the world, minorities with virtually no political power or other means of discriminating against the majority population have nevertheless been far more successful—economically, educationally, or otherwise— than those who constitute the bulk of the nation's people," he wrote. "This has long been true of the Chinese in Malaysia, Indonesia, and the Philippines, Germans in Russia and Brazil, Jews in Eastern Europe and the United States, Lebanese in West Africa, Scots in North America and Australia, and the Japanese in Brazil, Canada, the United States, and Peru. Clearly, in these and other cases, the minority has simply outperformed the majority population, often in both the educational system and the economic system."[8]

Sowell brought an entirely different set of expectations to these inequality debates, often because he had an entirely different conception of the underlying problem. And a proper understanding of his starting point is integral to understanding his sizable body of work on race, ethnicity, and culture. Others make assumptions that Sowell did not; indeed, the rejection of unproven assumptions may be the most distinguishing feature of his analyses. This characteristic was evident in his response in a 1990 television interview when he was asked why "different parts of society do better than others":

> I would look at it differently. I would say—and especially in the United States, I would say: "Why would we expect different groups to do the same?" I say, "especially in the United States," because there are very few indigenous Americans. Americans have come here from all over the world. And why would you ever expect that countries that had entirely different histories—located in entirely different climates, different geographies—why would you expect those countries to develop exactly the same mix of skills, to exactly the same degree, so that their people would arrive on these shores in such a way that they would be represented evenly across the board? Especially since even in countries where most of the population is indigenous, you don't find it there. . . . Nowhere in the world do you find this evenness that people use as

a norm. And I find it fascinating that they will hold up as a norm something that has never been seen on this planet, and regard as an anomaly something that is seen in country after country.[9]

The cultural trilogy that Sowell released in the 1990s began as one large manuscript that ran to more than a thousand pages before he decided to break it up into separate books. Collectively, he said, these works were intended to answer "one of the most fundamental questions: Why are there such vast disparities in income and wealth, among racial and ethnic groups, among nations and among civilizations?"[10] People with different ideologies of course tend to have different explanations for social inequality in America and elsewhere. Broadly speaking, one side blames external factors, such as discrimination and exploitation. The other side points to the uneven development of human capital among various races and ethnicities. Sowell wanted to test these explanations empirically, and he showed that the assumptions you bring to the discussion can make all the difference in how you interpret the results.

Race and Culture: A World View, published in 1994, was the first book in the trilogy and a summary of his findings. Indeed, it summarized a professional lifetime of research into what best explains the differing racial and ethnic group outcomes, both within countries and between them. Together, the books assessed the roles that everything from geography and climate to war, slavery, economics, and politics have played in human advancement. Most analyses of social and economic intergroup differences focus on the immediate surroundings in which people live. Sowell's writings exposed the limitations of that approach.

He concluded that it isn't the immediate environment per se, but cultural values and human capital—skills, work habits, saving propensities, attitudes toward education and entrepreneurship, developed sometimes over long periods of time—that are the more dominant factors in explaining disparities. And a global assessment of these different cultural patterns, he said, is crucial to comprehending why that is:

> Group cultural patterns may indeed be products of environments—but often of environments that existed on the other side of an ocean, in the lives of ancestors long forgotten, yet transmitted over generations as distilled values, preferences, skills, and habits. The outward veneer of a new society—its language, dress, and customs—may mask these underlying differences in cultural values, which are nevertheless revealed when the hard choices of life have to be made, and sacrifices endured, to achieve competing goals.
>
> Where an analysis is confined to one society— racial and ethnic groups in the United States, for example—it can be difficult to establish which patterns are the result of the way particular groups were treated in American society and which are the results of their own internal cultural patterns. But where the analysis is international in scope, then the group patterns which recur in country after country can more readily be distinguished from historical differences in the group's experience from one country to another.[11]

In writing the trilogy, Sowell drew on vast amounts of research and international data to debunk the assumption that differences in the performance of racial and ethnic groups stem entirely, or even predominantly, from surrounding social structures. He was not trying to say that culture explains everything, or that cultures are permanent, but he did reject the "a priori dogma that all cultures are equal." Such relativism may be politically correct, he argued, but it's not supported by the evidence. And these books provide example after example of not only key cultural differences but how those differences have shaped the course of history, for better or worse. In *Conquests and Cultures*, for example, Sowell explained how the relative social isolation of indigenous Americans put them at a tremendous disadvantage when the Europeans arrived:

> The technology that the Europeans brought to the Western Hemisphere was not simply the technology of Europe. Because of the geography of the Eurasian land mass, Europeans were able to bring to bear in the Western Hemisphere the cultural features of lands extending far beyond Europe, but incorporated into their civilization. Europeans were able to cross the Atlantic Ocean in the first place because they could steer with rudders invented in China, calculate their positions on the open sea through trigonometry invented in Egypt, using numbers created in India. The knowledge they had accumulated from around the world was preserved in letters invented in China. The military power they brought with them increasingly depended on weapons using gunpowder, also invented in Asia. The cultural confrontation in the Western Hemisphere was, in effect, a one-sided struggle between cultures acquired from vast regions of

the earth against cultures from much more narrowly circumscribed regions of the New World. Never have the advantages of a wider cultural universe been more dramatically or more devastatingly demonstrated than in the conquests that followed.[12]

What today is disparaged by liberal progressives as "cultural appropriation" is more accurately described as borrowing and one-upmanship—without which there would be no human progress, Sowell argued. He wrote on this topic in *Race and Culture*:

> Whatever the nature of cultural competition, whether it is warfare or international trade, scientific break-throughs or the spread of popular music, competition means winners and losers. . . . Some may lament that colorful local fabrics in non-Western societies have been superseded by mass-produced cloth from the factories of Europe or the United States. They may regret seeing traditional local drinks replaced by car-bonated sodas, or indigenous musical instruments put aside while people listen to American popular songs on Japanese-made portable radios. Those who de-plore such things are also deploring the very process of cultural diffusion by which the human race has ad-vanced for thousands of years.[13]

But Sowell's overriding argument was that there is no reason to expect people from different racial and ethnic backgrounds to have similar outcomes in the first place. "In short, different peoples have lived in different cultural uni-verses, rooted in different histories, evolved from different imperatives," he wrote. "Understanding the nature and scope of the cultural universe is essential to understanding differences in the ways in which different peoples confront the same challenges and opportunities."[14]

THE SECOND-ORDER PROBLEM THAT SOWELL IDENTIFIED was the attempt by public policy makers to help lagging groups through programs such as affirmative action quotas and set-asides. These efforts were based on the mistaken assumption that equal or proportionate outcomes are normal, and that where we don't find them, something nefarious is afoot. "Intergroup differences have been the rule, not the exception, in countries around the world and throughout centuries of history," he wrote. "Today, one need only turn on the television set and watch a professional basketball game to see that the races are not evenly or randomly represented in this sport and are not in proportion to their representation in the general population of the United States. Racially, the teams do not 'look like America.'" Other examples abounded:

> Although not visible to the naked eye, neither do the beer companies that sponsor this and other athletic events. Most, if not all, of the leading beer-producing companies in the United States were founded by people of German ancestry. So were most of the leading piano manufacturers. Nor is German domination of these institutions limited to the United States.
>
> The kind of demographic over-representation in particular lines of work found among blacks in basketball or Germans in beer brewing and piano-making

can also be found among Jews in the apparel industry—not just in contemporary New York but also in the history of medieval Spain, the Ottoman Empire, the Russian Empire, Brazil, Germany and Chile. At one time, most of the clothing stores in Melbourne were owned by Jews, who have never been as much as one percent of the Australian population.[15]

The trilogy is rich with supporting examples and statistics. Sowell is intent on making empirical arguments and has a way of making the numbers almost sing. "It's respect for the data and it is respect for historical facts, but of course, the concept precedes the data," said George Gilder. "You never get the sense that Sowell is inundated by empirical data collection. He has a conceptual mastery that allows him to see the relevant numbers. That's why he's so effective. It's not that he's inductive. The idea comes before the data. For him, it just does."[16]

In the preface to *Race and Culture*, Sowell explained that the book was intended, first and foremost, to be analysis and not "to offer some grand theory explaining cultural differences." He is sometimes criticized, even by admirers, for not offering more in the way of solutions to the problems he identifies. But Sowell doesn't see that as his role and generally has been content to leave problem-solving to others. "This book deliberately offers little in the way of direct policy prescriptions, for its underlying premise is that what is most needed is an understanding of existing realities, the history from which the present evolved, and the enduring principles constraining our options for the future," he wrote. "There is seldom a shortage of people willing to draw up blueprints for salvation. What is important is that such people and those who judge their proposals both understand what they are talking about."[17]

Sowell wants to make his readers smarter, not tell them what to do. And in his constrained view of human nature, third parties are largely incapable of "fixing" the cultural differences that lead to unequal outcomes. What matters most is a group's self-development, to which there are no shortcuts. Moreover, there's little evidence that the progress of a race or ethnic group can be socially engineered. The best we can hope for are public policies that don't make the situation any worse and allow that necessary development to take place. "My theory of how to get rid of poverty is to hold a meeting of all the leading experts on poverty in the middle of the Pacific and not let them go home for 10 years," he once joked in an interview.[18]

This is the thinking behind Sowell's extensive writings on "affirmative action" over the past half-century. Even before racial preferences went by that name, he was skeptical of their efficacy and wary of the side effects. "Affirmative action calls into question the competency of all blacks by trying to help some blacks," he told me. Recall that as far back as the early 1960s, Sowell had denounced, on both tactical and moral grounds, efforts by civil rights leaders to seek special treatment for blacks. It was also a personal issue for him, a black man from the Jim Crow South. He is old enough to remember where he was when news broke that the Japanese had bombed Pearl Harbor. "I'm old-fashioned enough to be against [affirmative action] simply because it is wrong," he said in a 1986 letter to a Reagan administration official who had asked him for his thoughts on racial-preference policies. "Having been forced by birth to be on the receiving end of discrimination for many years, I cannot find the cleverness to justify discrimination now, either to others or to myself. And if I now reduce this issue to a pragmatic question of whose ox is gored, then what right did I have to be indignant before?"[19]

Perhaps Sowell has never been more indignant about affirmative action than he was after receiving a form letter in 1972 from the chairman of the economics department at Swarthmore College, who stated that he was "actively looking for a black economist" to hire. Sowell wrote back in no uncertain terms:

> What *purpose* is to be served by this sort of thing? . . . Surely a labor economist of your reputation must know that unemployment among black Ph.D.s is one of the least of our social problems, and has been for many years—long before "affirmative action." . . . Maybe you think you are doing something for race relations. If you are going to find Swarthmore-quality black faculty members, that is one thing. But Swarthmore-quality faculty members are found through Swarthmore-quality channels and not through mimeographed letters of this sort. Many a self-respecting black scholar would never accept an offer like this, even if he would enjoy teaching at Swarthmore otherwise. When Bill Allen was chairman at U.C.L.A. he violently refused to hire anyone on the basis of ethnic representation—and thereby made it possible for me to come there a year later with my head held up. Your approach tends to make the job unattractive to anyone who regards himself as a scholar or a man, and thereby throws it open to opportunists.

Despite all the brave talk in academia about "affirmative action" without lowering standards, you and I both know that it takes many years to create qualified faculty members of any color, and no increased demand is going to immediately increase the supply *unless* you lower quality. Now what good is going to come from lower standards that will make "black" equivalent to "substandard" in the eyes of black and white students alike?[20]

The start of Sowell's career in academia in the early 1960s predated the implementation of racial preferences in hiring, and in his memoirs he recounted how, over time, these policies changed the way he was perceived by both colleagues and students. "One of the ironies that I experienced in my own career was that I received more automatic respect when I first began teaching in 1962, as an inexperienced young man with no Ph.D. and few publications, than later on in the 1970s, after accumulating a more substantial record," he wrote. "What happened in between was 'affirmative action' hiring of minority faculty." At UCLA, where he taught in the 1970s, students would sometimes approach him at the end of the semester to express their appreciation of the class, but "there was often some revealing phrase to let me know they had been pleasantly surprised," he said. He provided an example:

One young man, early in the term, came to me with a question about a passage in the textbook that he was having difficulty understanding. After I explained what it meant, he asked:

"Are you sure?"

"Yes, I'm sure," I said. "I wrote the textbook."

He then noticed my name on the cover and was obviously embarrassed. It was one of the signs of the time, one of the fruits of "affirmative action."[21]

Sowell has given the subject of group preferences his most extensive treatment in *The Economics and Politics of Race, Civil Rights: Rhetoric or Reality?, Preferential Policies, Race and Culture*, and *Affirmative Action Around the World*, as well as in numerous columns and longer essays over the decades. He has written about the origins of racial preferences, their impact on hiring decisions, and their role in college admissions. He has questioned their very necessity and argued that in practice they can undermine self-development and serve to diminish the accomplishments of successful blacks. He's mulled the legality of racial double-standards and the wisdom of creating a racial spoils system in an increasingly pluralistic society. He's written about how racial preferences have affected not only blacks and Hispanics but also Asians and women. He's noted how they started as efforts to ensure equal opportunity without regard to race, but evolved into numerical goals and quotas; how they were supposed to be temporary, but became open-ended; and how they have been sold as efforts to help the poor, but in practice have helped those who were already better off to begin with. He has shown how the justification for preferences inevitably changes over time and critiqued the rationale for using them as a means of historical redress. And, of course, Sowell has shown how none of this is unique to affirmative action policies in the United States, but in fact has been the pattern in country after country all over the world. The preface to his 1990 book, *Preferential Policies: An International Perspective*, begins with a choice anecdote:

> The international nature of the issue of preferential policies was unintentionally dramatized for me one evening by a well-educated Maori woman who was part of a group having dinner together in an expensive restaurant in Auckland, New Zealand. The central theme of her explicit argument was the historical uniqueness of the Maoris in New Zealand—and how that uniqueness justified and required preferential policies. But the key concepts she used, her general attitude, the intonations of her voice, her facial expressions and gestures, the body language, the buzzwords, her evasive, accusatory, and retaliatory responses to any serious questions or criticisms, all could have been found in almost any large city in the United States, among the representatives of any of a long list of groups having or seeking preferential treatment. With local variations, similar arguments and attitudes can be encountered from Britain to Malaysia to Fiji, and at many points in between. Whatever the uniqueness of the Maoris in New Zealand, the arguments and connotations were closer to being universal than unique.[22]

In Sowell's dissident view, affirmative action is yet another misguided policy "solution" to a misdiagnosed problem. Advocates presume that something approaching statistical parity in outcomes is normal—that if women are around 47 percent of the workforce, but constitute a much lower percentage of law firm partners or US senators or Fortune 500 chief executives, then gender discrimination must be the reason. Sowell rejected that thinking, not because he believed sexism was nonexistent, but because correlation is not causation, and the empirical evidence showed that other explanations for gender disparities in the labor market were far more plausible. What has also distinguished Sowell's writings in this area is that he has been much less concerned with the intentions behind such policies than with analyzing the actual results that have followed their implementation.

His definitive work on group preferences, *Affirmative Action Around the World: An Empirical Study* (2004), is a devastating cost-benefit analysis of just how often these policies have failed to achieve their stated goals. Sowell explains that the trade-offs associated with affirmative action are seldom scrutinized but nevertheless significant. "Among the costs are lowered standards of performance in order to get numerical results," he wrote. "Moreover, these standards are sometimes lowered for all, in order to avoid the political embarrassment or legal liability of obvious double standards for favored groups." Sowell also points out that preference policies have been used to create a false sense of dependency, insofar as underrepresented groups are led to believe that special treatment is necessary in order for them to advance. "In addition to the hostilities between groups created or exacerbated by preferences and quotas in other countries, affirmative action in the United States has made blacks, who have largely lifted themselves out of poverty, look like people who owe their rise to affirmative action and other government programs," he observed. "Moreover, this perception is not confined to whites. It has been carefully cultivated by black politicians and civil rights leaders, who seek to claim credit for the progress, so as to solidify a constituency conditioned to be dependent on them, as well as on government."[23]

SOWELL'S MISGIVINGS ABOUT AFFIRMATIVE ACTION POLI-cies and the various justifications used to keep them in place date back decades, but his critiques remain as timely as ever. In recent years, Ivy League institutions have been sued for allegedly capping Asian enrollment by holding Asian applicants to higher standards than other groups. High schools for gifted students have come under pressure to drop their testing requirements for admission, owing to racial disparities in exam results. Revisionist dogma claiming that the American Revolution was fought to pre-serve slavery, and that racially disparate outcomes today are a direct legacy of that institution, is being promoted by the *New York Times* and taught in elementary schools across the country. Black Lives Matter activists and other civil rights groups have abandoned any pretense of color-blindness and pressed for race-based remedies to address inequality. Perhaps most disturbingly, the debate over slav-ery reparations not only continues but has gained promi-nent advocates.

In 2019, the best-selling author Ta-Nehisi Coates tes-tified before Congress in support of slavery reparations for blacks. He began his remarks with a discussion of what he termed America's "inheritance of slavery." Although slaves and slaveholders are long gone, he said, Americans living today are still "bound to a collective enterprise that extends beyond our individual and personal reach." He added, "We recognize our lineage as a generational trust, as inheritance, and the real dilemma posed by reparations is just that: a dilemma of inheritance," citing heavily disputed calculations of slavery's contribution to American prosperity.[24] Coates went on to assert a direct causal link between the past suffering of blacks and racial disparities today:

> Enslavement reigned for 250 years on these shores. When it ended, this country could have extended its hallowed principles—life, liberty, and the pursuit of happiness—to all, regardless of color. But America had other principles in mind. And so for a century after the Civil War, black people were subjected to a relentless campaign of terror . . .
>
> It is tempting to divorce this modern campaign of terror, of plunder, from enslavement, but the logic of enslavement, of white supremacy, respects no such borders and the guard of bondage was lustful and begat many heirs. Coup d'états and convict leasing. Vagrancy laws and debt peonage. Redlining and racist G.I. bills. Poll taxes and state-sponsored terrorism. . . .
>
> . . . It was 150 years ago. And it was right now.
>
> The typical black family in this country has one-tenth the wealth of the typical white family.[25]

Other witnesses that day testified in opposition to slavery reparations, and they could have done much worse than simply to have read aloud a couple of pages of Tom Sowell, who some three decades earlier, in his 1990 book *Preferential Policies*, had not only anticipated Coates's arguments with eerie precision but also addressed the underlying assumptions and sloppy reasoning used to support them:

> The wrongs of history have been invoked by many groups in many countries as a moral claim for contemporary compensation. Much emotional fervor goes into such claims but the question here is about their logic or morality. Assuming for the sake of argument that the historical claims are factually correct, which may not be the case in all countries, to transfer benefits between two groups of living contemporaries because of what happened between two sets of dead people is to raise the question whether any sufferer is in fact being compensated. Only where both wrongs and compensation are viewed as collectivized and inheritable does redressing the wrongs of history have a moral, or even a logical basis.
>
> The biological continuity of the generations lends plausibility to the notion of group compensation—but only if guilt can be inherited. Otherwise there are simply windfall gains and windfall losses among contemporaries, according to the accident of their antecedents. Moreover, few people would accept this as a general principle to be applied consistently, however much they may advocate it out of compassion (or guilt) over the fate of particular unfortunates. No one would advocate that today's Jews are morally entitled to put today's Germans in concentration camps, in compensation for the Nazi Holocaust. Most people would not only be horrified at any such suggestion but would also regard it as a second act of gross

immorality, in no way compensating for the first, but simply adding to the sum total of human sins.

Sowell also warned against assuming that the "contemporary troubles of historically wronged groups are due to those wrongs," which may be tempting to do but needs to be demonstrated empirically, not merely asserted:

The contemporary socioeconomic position of groups in a given society often bears no relationship to the historic wrongs they have suffered. Both in Canada and the United States, the Japanese have significantly higher incomes than the whites, who have a documented history of severe anti-Japanese discrimination in both countries. The same story could be told of the Chinese in Malaysia, Indonesia, and many other countries around the world, of the Jews in countries with virulent anti-Semitism, and a wide variety of groups in a wide variety of other countries. Among poorer groups as well, the level of poverty often has little correlation with the degree of oppression. No one would claim that the historic wrongs suffered by Puerto Ricans in the United States exceed those suffered by blacks, but the average Puerto Rican income is lower than the average income of blacks.

None of this proves that historic wrongs have no contemporary effects. Rather, it is a statement about the limitations of our knowledge, which is grossly inadequate to the task undertaken and likely to remain so. To pretend to disentangle the innumerable sources of intergroup differences is an exercise in hubris rather than morality.[26]

It's also a statement on just how long Sowell has been thinking circles around people who have received far more attention and praise than would seem warranted.

PENETRATING SCHOLARLY ASSESSMENTS OF SOWELL'S WRIT-ings on cultural issues are hard to come by; the assessments that do exist don't tend to penetrate very far. That's especially true among his black critics, who can seldom be counted on to grapple with his ideas. Instead, they often accuse him of racial betrayal, regardless of the strength of his arguments or his ability to back them up with facts, data, and logic. Independent thinking on racial controversies does not simply go unrewarded in academia and the media. Black contrarians are often vilified and ostracized by other blacks. They are expected to think a certain way about race and inequality, and those who do not can find themselves dismissed as not "really" black. In his 1984 book, *The Myth of Black Progress*, the sociologist Alphonso Pinkney accuses Sowell types of espousing views that undermine black intellectual solidarity. "Black social scientists, as well as white, appear to be supporting the growing conservative movement in the United States," said Pinkney. "That white social scientists should engage in these activities is not surprising. However, black sociologists who support the conservative movement are not unlike government officials in (formerly) South Vietnam who supported American aggression against their own people."[27]

Sowell's problem with such thinking was not simply that he'd always been someone who marched to his own drummer. "Self-respect is the most important thing," he's written. "Without it, the world's adulation rings hollow. And with it, even venomous attacks are like water off a duck's back."[28] His larger concern was that, as a scholar, he rejected on empirical grounds the premise that minority-group cohesiveness was a prerequisite for economic advancement. Pinkney said that blacks needed to stick together politically and ideologically. Sowell's response was that if thinking in lockstep works, show me the evidence. "Ethnic identity has sometimes been thought to be a potent—if not paramount—factor in group progress," wrote Sowell. "But groups with much group identity—in such things as bloc voting or favoritism for political candidates or employees of one's own ethnicity—have not generally done better than groups with less concern over such things."[29]

Indeed, he'd argued that lockstep thinking can be counterproductive and that we shouldn't assume that the benefits of solidarity would exceed their costs. "Group-think does not always lead to wiser decisions than what emerges from a clash of differing individual ideas from within and beyond the group," he wrote. "More dangerously, group solidarity often means letting the lowest common denominator shape the culture and life within the group and determine the direction of its future. This can range from black students being accused of 'acting white' for being conscientious about their studies to automatic criticisms of police actions against rioters or criminals. These are self-inflicted wounds that can jeopardize the whole future of a people."[30]

When I asked Sowell about the criticism of his methodology and his independence, he was unapologetic. "I imagine the Pony Express reacted that way to Western Union's methods," he quipped. "No horses." He said he didn't spend a lot of time worrying about such lines of attack: "It's not something that concerns me much because when all is said and done, it's a question of evidence and logic. If they are experts in those fields, they should have better evidence and logic than I have. And if they can't manage to do that, then the mere fact that they are poohbahs in their field doesn't mean much." There's "no a priori reason to say that what's happened here [in America] is unique," and can't be compared to what's happened to other people in other places at other times. "It's a question of whether and to what extent other countries' situations are similar and different. And it can only be investigated empirically." This debate, he added, "was part of a wider issue that [Milton] Friedman dealt with long ago—the problem of descriptive accuracy versus analytical relevance. Descriptively, it's true that these groups are different. The question is whether, as you proceed to analyze, your conclusions are supportable by the evidence."[31]

Sowell also told me that he found suspect the whole idea of a need for racial and ethnic leadership. "One of the things that struck me domestically as well as internationally among groups that have risen from poverty to affluence is that they almost never have so-called leaders of the prominence of those groups that remain lagging," he said. "Who has been able to take credit for the Jews rising or for the Asian Americans? Where is their Martin Luther King?"[32]

ON ONE LEVEL, IT COULD BE SAID THAT SOWELL AND HIS detractors were talking past one another. Critics offered evidence that racism still existed and then insisted that its existence was a satisfactory explanation for racial gaps in wealth, employment, incarceration rates, and other areas. Sowell countered with examples of ethnic and racial minorities that had faced discrimination but nevertheless were able to rise out of difficult circumstances, and sometimes outperform the very groups that had discriminated against them. To him, this data showed that the existence of racism was an insufficient explanation of social inequality. To his critics, it showed that intergroup comparisons are imperfect, and therefore invalid, and that the black American experience is sui generis.

So much criticism of Sowell over the decades has amounted to name-calling and pop-psychoanalysis disguised as scholarly scrutiny that it's easy to miss the rare but more serious attempts to take on his ideas. Thomas D. Boston's *Race, Class and Conservatism*, published in 1988, endeavored to do just that.[33] Boston, an economist at Georgia Tech, aimed to show that job discrimination was still a reality and that Sowell's belief in market competition to address income gaps was misplaced. But even in this assessment, by an academic peer acting in good faith and with all the accompanying data and charts and jargon, there is no real pushback against Sowell's underlying argument. Boston succeeds in showing that racial discrimination in labor markets still exists, but that is something Sowell hasn't denied. What Boston doesn't show is that past or existing discrimination is the *main cause* of white-black gaps in employment and income, which is what he would need to show in order to address Sowell's thesis head-on.

The post-1960s era saw a dramatic *decline* in laborforce participation among black men, which represented a significant reversal from what had been occurring in the

1940s and 1950s. Boston's argument is that racial discrimination is the *main culprit*, which is certainly possible. But is it plausible? Does anyone seriously believe that black outcomes in the labor force began to worsen dramatically in the 1970s and 1980s because of an *increase* in racial discrimination during that period? If Boston wanted to posit that racism primarily drove racial gaps in the labor force, he would have needed to present empirical evidence that racism had been increasing. His book provides no such evidence. Sowell, on the other hand, presents ample data showing that factors other than discrimination were more likely responsible for an increase in the size of the black underclass. Boston doesn't present an empirically based counterargument to that; instead, he asks readers to accept his own evidence-free inferences that racial bias alone largely explains today's racial disparities.

It's hard not to conclude that Sowell has spent a career being hounded by media and intellectuals who are mediocrities by comparison. This is especially true with regard to liberal black critics of his writings on race who can match neither his scholarly range nor his depth of analysis. "A *New York Times* book review said he was the most prominent black social scientist in America," said Tom Hazlett, a professor of economics who knows Sowell personally and has used his books in classes over the years. "That was in 1980. I remember that line. What are you going to do if you're on the left and you're an intellectual and you want to say that Cornel West is the cat's meow? If we put those guys at the same table, it's not that they're different. It's that Sowell really is at a whole different level. It's not a fair fight."[34]

Another tactic of Sowell's critics has been to simply ignore him, to pretend that there is no other way for black people to think about racial gaps in America. When I asked William B. Allen, a black political scientist and former chairman of the United States Commission on Civil Rights, what he made of how the black left has treated Sowell and his scholarship on race and ethnicity, he was amused by the question. "Well, what can you make of silence?" he answered. "That's largely been the response. They do not engage Tom. They dismiss Tom without consideration, in general, so one cannot make a great deal out of that other than the fact that they are unwilling to enter into the risks." Allen said there's been "no sustained criticism of Tom" from liberal black intellectuals and writers. "There has been glancing criticism here and there that I've seen over the years, but never anyone taking him up seriously from the left."[35]

Walter Williams, Sowell's friend of fifty years, who died in 2020, agreed. Williams was a black economist at George Mason University who was also known for writing a popular syndicated column with a libertarian bent. The two men met when Sowell was teaching at UCLA and Williams was earning his PhD there under the guidance of James Buchanan. Williams never took any of Sowell's classes, but when he got word that there was a black faculty member who shared his views, he sought Sowell out and introduced himself. In the 1980s, they joked that they never flew together, because if the plane went down there would be no black conservatives left.

Williams told me that the lack of engagement of Sowell's ideas among black liberals makes sense when you understand that it is not in their interests to draw attention to the types of things Sowell is saying. Black activists such as Jesse Jackson and Al Sharpton, and black intellectuals such as Cornel West, Henry Louis Gates Jr., and Ta-Nehisi Coates, he said, "benefit immensely from making white people feel guilty. But Tom does not benefit from making white people feel guilty and neither do I, so they don't have any use for us. What we say acts against those interests, so they don't engage."[36]

In his autobiography, *Up from the Projects*, Williams recounted columnist Carl Rowan's reaction to watching Sowell explain, on television, how minimum-wage laws had harmed the job prospects of younger blacks. Rowan didn't respond with a column that cited empirical studies proving Sowell wrong. His response was emotional: "Vidkun Quisling, in his collaboration with the Nazis, surely did not do as much damage to the Norwegians as Sowell is doing to the most helpless of black Americans. Sowell is giving aid and comfort to America's racists and to those who, in the name of conservatism and frugality, are taking the food out of the mouths of black children, consigning hundreds of thousands of black teenagers to joblessness and hopelessness . . ."

Rowan could not discredit the argument, so he attempted to discredit the person making the argument. "Rowan was obviously oblivious to the broad consensus among academic economists that the minimum wage law discriminates against the employment of low-skill workers, who are disproportionately black teenagers," wrote Williams, who distinguished himself in the mid-1970s through research on how wage mandates impacted minority unemployment rates. "Indeed, a 1976 survey by the

American Economic Association found that 90 percent of its members agreed that increasing the minimum wage increases unemployment among the young and unskilled. A subsequent survey, in 1990, found 80 percent of economists agreeing with the proposition that increases in the minimum wage cause unemployment among the youth and low skilled."[37]

Sowell was not the only black conservative on the receiving end of hysterical attacks, but in the 1970s and 1980s he was easily the most prominent one, which means he bore the brunt of the criticism. "I remember the first time I got accused of selling out," he told me. "It was some black militant at Cornell. I'm living there with my little family in the upstairs of a two-bedroom duplex apartment, driving a Volkswagen bug. He had a house with two Mercedes parked out front."

Sowell said that in some ways he finds the vitriol reassuring, because it demonstrates that his critics have no substantive arguments to offer. "I'm often amazed for someone who writes about so many controversial issues—not just race—how little real criticism I get. People ask what the civil rights groups say in response. They say nothing. And that's their strategy. They cannot engage. There are people who do engage, but the people on the other side do not."[38]

9

SOWELL MAN

"Sometimes it seems as if I have spent the
first half of my life refusing to let white
people define me and the second half
refusing to let black people define me."[1]

OVER THE DECADES THOMAS SOWELL HAS GROWN ACCUS-
tomed to a certain type of media query, usually from white
interviewers. They want to know how, as a black conservative thinker, he has dealt with all the criticism coming from
fellow blacks. Sometimes the question is direct, as when
Charlie Rose once asked him: "How was it, though, for
you—and I've watched you and read you for years—to be
an African American man respected by a cross section of
your peers and yet be so against the grain of fellow African
Americans?" Other times, the questioner tries to be more
circumspect, at least at first. C-SPAN's Brian Lamb once
read aloud a passage from Sowell's *Preferential Policies:
An International Perspective* on how minorities who are
skeptical of affirmative action have been labeled traitors
to their race, and then asked the author, "Were you talking
about yourself?" In either case, these inquiries represent a

certain fascination with the psychology of being Thomas Sowell. They want to analyze this oddity, put him on the couch.

Sowell's habit is to respond to this line of inquiry by challenging the premise. "I don't know if we can say [that I go] 'against the grain of fellow African Americans,'" he told Rose. "You mean fellow African American *intellectuals*. But I don't think African American intellectuals are any more typical of African Americans than white intellectuals are of whites."[2] His answer to Lamb wound up being more elaborate. Yes, said Sowell, he himself is one of many examples of people in countries around the world whose criticisms of preferential policies have been met with charges of racial or ethnic disloyalty. But Lamb pressed him further: "Is there a way for you to put in a nutshell" what people of "your own race say . . . about you?"

At which point Sowell cut him off. "Oh, wait, wait. I think one of the ways that the organized noisemakers have succeeded is saying that what they're saying is what their race is saying," he said. "My *race* is not saying that about me. *Those particular individuals, who are a small minority themselves within the black community—who have a vested interest in many of these [affirmative action] programs—they are saying that*" (emphasis added). Sowell told Lamb that black strangers regularly stop him in public and compliment him for his views. They have read his books and columns, or seen him on television, and agree with what he has to say: "When I checked out of my hotel this morning, the black security guard came over and said, 'Are you Sowell?' And I said, 'Yes,' and he shook my hand warmly and we walked—he walked me the length of the corridor and talked about this and about that—and that's not at all an uncommon experience for me. So, it's not Sowell versus blacks. It's the black intellectuals." He further explained to Lamb that these intellectuals "have a very large, vested interest in certain beliefs, which underlie various programs from which they benefit enormously. And, as I point out in the book, this is common around the world, that the elites benefit from preferential programs."[3]

Indeed, there is a long history of conflating the interests of most black Americans with the interests of black organizations, black journalists, black academics, and other black elites who profess to advocate on their behalf. And the media lazily continue to turn to these groups, from the NAACP to Black Lives Matter, asking them to speak for all black people, thus becoming a large part of the phenomenon that Sowell identified. As far back as 1965, William Raspberry—who later became a widely read syndicated columnist, but at the time was a cub reporter for the *Washington Post*—noted the sizable disconnect between the priorities of the black leadership and those of the black rank-and-file:

> Civil Rights progress, remarkable as it has been in recent years, has bypassed poor Negroes. In the North especially, most civil rights gains have benefited the Negro middle class and left the disadvantaged masses largely unaffected. This is particularly true in Washington, where a majority of the population is Negro . . .
>
> "When the District passes a law barring discrimination in the sale of housing, that's progress all right," says Roena Rand, chairman of Washington's

Congress of Racial Equality. "But it doesn't mean a thing to the little guy who can't afford to buy a house in the first place." . . .

The same is true of other civil rights gains, such as opening of top-level jobs and desegregation of posh restaurants. Negroes who weren't doing badly to begin with are doing even better, while those at the bottom stay there. The result is a growing sense of frustration and hopelessness on the part of the un-skilled, unlettered, and jobless slum dwellers as they see themselves falling farther and farther behind both whites and middle-class Negroes.[4]

Robert Woodson is a black community activist who broke with traditional black leaders in the 1970s over the issue of school busing and the civil rights leadership's broader emphasis on racial integration as a cure for in-equality. "The left assumes that if you're not for forced integration, then you support segregation, but that's a false dichotomy," he told the *Wall Street Journal* in 2014. "I be-lieve we should have fought for desegregation, but forced integration is a separate issue, especially in education." A majority of black parents always opposed this method of social engineering and said they wanted better neighbor-hood schools, "but the civil-rights leadership pushed bus-ing for the poor. Of course, none of their kids were on the bus," said Woodson.[5] In a 1998 book, Woodson described how the "split between the demands of the leaders of the civil rights establishment and the concerns of their pur-ported constituents," on any number of issues, had wid-ened since the 1960s. In one of the book's more remarkable passages, Woodson contrasted the contemporary attitudes of the black public with those of black leaders:

> In one survey . . . conducted by the Joint Center for Political and Economic Studies, 83 percent of black respondents who knew about school vouchers said they were in favor of choice programs "where parents can send their children to any public or private school that will accept them." Yet in a floor vote at the 1993 NAACP convention, delegates passed a resolution opposing voucher programs that would provide low-income children with the means to attend private schools. When *Washington Post* pollsters asked whether minorities should receive preferential treatment to make up for past discrimination, 77 percent of black leaders said yes, while 77 percent of the black public said no. . . . Another survey of the black population taken by a research group, Fabrizio, McLaughlin, and Associates, in 1993 revealed that 91 percent of the respondents were in favor of requiring able-bodied welfare recipients to work for their benefits and 59 percent favored eliminating parole for repeat violent offenders.[6]

According to Woodson, the controversy over the appointment of Clarence Thomas to the Supreme Court in 1991 could be viewed as a "nationwide referendum of blacks regarding the values and goals that should guide the black community." Thomas's message of personal responsibility, as well as his focus on equal opportunity rather than equal outcomes, "resonated with grassroots blacks,"

Woodson wrote. "Polls consistently revealed that the majority of the black populace supported Thomas's nomination and that the lower the income level, the greater the support. At the same time, Clarence Thomas's greatest antagonists were leaders of the civil rights establishment who viewed his positions as a threat to their agenda of race-based grievances."[7]

THOMAS SOWELL HAS NOT GAINED ICONIC STATUS BY GOING "against the grain" of most blacks. Rather, he's done so by taking on the thinking of most black intellectuals. If Charlie Rose and Brian Lamb didn't fully appreciate the distinction, that is by design. The black intelligentsia has long been preoccupied with guarding the public image of the race. The practical needs of everyday blacks often have been treated as a secondary concern. In his 1962 essay "The Failure of the Negro Intellectual," the sociologist E. Franklin Frazier noted that the black intellectual "has carried on all sorts of arguments in defense of the Negro but they were mainly designed to protect his own status and soothe his hurt self-esteem."[8]

Sowell would pick up on this theme nearly two decades later in a pair of explosive *Washington Post* op-eds—"Blacker Than Thou" and "Blacker Than Thou (II)"—published in 1981. In these articles he described the internal social history of black Americans—which included discrimination by lighter-skinned blacks against darker-skinned blacks—and how that history had influenced the makeup and priorities of today's black elite. He also described the snobbishness of black leaders, from W. E. B. Du Bois to Andrew Young, toward the black masses in whose name they spoke. "Historically, the black elite has been preoccupied with symbolism rather than pragmatism," he wrote. "Like other human beings, they have been able to rationalize their special perspective and self-interest as a general good. Much of their demand for removing racial barriers was a demand that they be allowed to join the white elite and escape the black masses."[9]

Sowell said that the civil rights establishment's hardwon victories against Jim Crow policies were essential to black progress and should never be forgotten. But he also said we can't assume that the priorities of groups like the NAACP and those of most black Americans will forever align going forward:

> Black "leadership" in general does not depend on expressing the opinions of blacks but on having access to whites—in the media, in politics and in philanthropy. Whites who have a limited time to give the problems of blacks need a few familiar blacks they can turn to. The civil rights organizations provide that convenience. . . .
>
> For the moment, the conventional black leadership has a virtual monopoly on expressing what blacks are supposed to believe. But it is an insecure monopoly. It is vulnerable to exposure to the truth.[10]

In the second *Post* op-ed, Sowell explained how these leaders have manipulated the media into believing that their thinking is typical of how all blacks see matters. "Those of us who take a different economic or political view—people like [the black libertarian economist] Walter Williams or myself—are grilled about our backgrounds by reporters who suspect we are middle-class, because we disagree with those whom the press has blindly accepted as the voice of blacks," he wrote. "The old elite is very good at playing on media conceptions, especially when they have run out of substantive arguments."[11]

In his memoir, Sowell said that these two columns caused the biggest uproar of anything he'd ever written, before or since, and he suspected that it was not so much because of what he had said, but because of where it had appeared—in a newspaper read by people who were well aware of internal color discrimination. "There was no way to deny it, especially not in Washington, where so many blacks knew about such things from their own personal experience," he wrote. "Denial being impossible, their anger at me for telling this dirty little secret took the form of venomous attacks which took up a whole page of the *Washington Post*—and I was also denounced for these articles in other publications that were likewise unable to deny the truth of what I had said."[12]

Even scholars otherwise in good standing on the political left have felt the wrath of black elites for deigning to challenge their perspective on racial controversies. In a 1989 *Harvard Law Review* article, the black legal scholar Randall Kennedy criticized the "empirical weakness and inflated rhetoric" of neo-Marxist critical race scholarship, which attributes social inequality to racial power structures.[13] Kennedy described how he was urged by fellow minority academics who read early drafts of the article not to air such views publicly. "I have been advised—in some cases warned—to forgo publishing the Article because, among other things, it will be put to bad use by enemies of racial justice," he wrote. "Second, they argue that my comments . . . are hostile to affirmative action insofar as they throw into doubt certain ideas that have been mobilized in favor of racial preferences in faculty hiring, particularly the notion that race should serve as a positive intellectual credential for minority scholars. Furthermore, it has been intimated that, given my status as a black scholar, publishing the Article shows a special lack of political responsibility."[14]

Kennedy said he felt a scholarly duty to publish the article anyway. "One must also consider the consequences of remaining silent in the face of analyses one believes to be wrong and misleading in important respects," he wrote. "Avoiding a public challenge to the racial critiques I have focused upon facilitates acceptance of theories and styles of thought that are seriously flawed, detrimental in effect, but nonetheless influential within important sectors of legal academia. In this case, keeping quiet is far more damaging than taking the risk that some of my ideas will be misappropriated."[15]

The sociologist William Julius Wilson is another black scholar who was chastised by other black elites for merely suggesting that racism, in and of itself, was an insufficient explanation for racial disparities. His 1978 book, *The Declining Significance of Race*, argued that the country's changing economic structure—factories moving out of cities and depriving lesser-skilled blacks of job opportunities, for example—had displaced racial discrimination as the main reason poorer blacks had been left behind. Some blacks were getting ahead while others were not, which suggested to Wilson that upward mobility had more to do with a person's social class than with his race. The book was well received by the general public and garnered positive reviews in mainstream media outlets, but its thesis riled the black intelligentsia. Like Kennedy, some accused the author of racial treachery. Wilson's analysis, wrote one black academic, was "from the perspective of the dominant people of power" and "cancels out racial discrimination as a key cause of poverty among blacks."[16]

Wilson argued that although affirmative action and other race-based policies were aimed at the poor, in practice they largely helped the black middle class, and other types of policies were necessary to address the stagnation of the most impoverished. Even critics who conceded Wilson's point about growing inequality among black Americans nevertheless hammered him for expressing these views publicly and straying from the focus on racism as a blanket explanation for societal disparities. To many of his black colleagues in academia, the veracity of Wilson's argument was less important than group cohesion and keeping the focus on white oppression. "The new emphasis on class, which was most clearly articulated in Wilson's *Declining Significance of Race*," wrote another black critic, "provided conservatives a fresh camouflage to hide their antipathy for social policies behind a concern for the growing class division in black society."[17]

IN 1980, A MONTH AFTER RONALD REAGAN'S ELECTION, Sowell headlined the "Black Alternatives" conference at the Fairmont Hotel in San Francisco. The media typically portrayed blacks as speaking with one voice on race policy. The goal of the conference was to showcase the variety of perspectives among black politicians, intellectuals, and activists. Future Supreme Court justice Clarence Thomas participated, as did the black economists Glenn Loury and Walter Williams. There were also black Democratic officials in attendance, such as Percy Sutton, a lawyer and prominent civil rights activist, and Charles V. Hamilton, a political scientist at Columbia University. Sowell gave the keynote address. "The people who were invited," he began, "are people who are seeking alternatives, people who have challenged the conventional wisdom on one or more issues, people who have thought for themselves instead of marching in step and chanting familiar refrains. . . . We have come through a historic phase of struggle for basic civil rights—a very necessary struggle, but not sufficient. The very success of that struggle has created new priorities and new urgencies. There are economic realities to confront and self-development to achieve, in the schools, at work, in our communities."

Then, as now, forty years later, liberal elites placed the onus on whites to fix the problems of blacks. Newer movements like Black Lives Matter, and younger public intellectuals such as Ta-Nehisi Coates and the critical race theorist Ibram X. Kendi, remain far more interested in white behavior than in black behavior. Sowell took a different approach. "The sins of others are always fascinating to human beings, but they are not always the best way to self-development or self-advancement," he said. "The moral regeneration of white people might be an interesting project, but I am not sure we have quite that much time to spare. Those who have fought on this front are very much like the generals who like to refight the last war instead of preparing for the next struggle."[18]

The event received extensive press coverage, and there were plans to put on a second conference and establish an organization that would promote perspectives different from those of the civil rights old guard. Ultimately, these plans faltered as a result of internal disagreements on how to proceed. Sowell also began to realize that the amount of work required to set up such an entity would take too much time away from his research and writing. We will never know how such an organization might have fared, but it's probably not a coincidence that the "Black Alternatives" conference took place when it did. Beginning in the late 1970s, a dozen or so serious black thinkers gained attention for challenging various aspects of the civil rights agenda that had emerged in the 1960s. On a few issues at least, Sowell seemed at the time to be gaining some black intellectual allies.

In addition to Randall Kennedy and William Julius Wilson, these allies included Clarence Thomas, Shelby Steele, Glenn Loury, Walter Williams, Stephen Carter, Orlando Patterson, Stanley Crouch, Anne Wortham, and Robert Woodson. During this period, the media would refer to these individuals as "black conservatives" or "black neoconservatives," although the labels didn't really apply to all of them in any meaningful ideological sense. Kennedy, for example, was certainly open-minded on some racial issues, but he was always firmly entrenched on the political left. Wilson was a European-style social democrat who employed neo-Marxian methodologies in his analyses of racial disparities, and the writings of Wortham and Williams had a strong libertarian bent. The "conservative" and "neoconservative" terms were used as a kind of shorthand to describe any black intellectual who had taken a position on a racial or cultural topic that ran contrary to the received wisdom among their fellow black elites. Steele, Carter, and Thomas had criticized racial preferences. Woodson had opposed busing. Patterson, Crouch, and Loury had denounced both the self-defeating behavior on display in black ghettoes and the civil rights leaders who specialized in making excuses for it. "The street culture of petty crime, drug addiction, paternal irresponsibility, whoring, pimping and super-fly inanity, all of which damage and destroy only fellow blacks, instead of being condemned by black ethnic leaders has, until recently, been hailed as the embodiment of black soul," wrote Patterson.[19]

Loury, a product of Chicago's notorious South Side, was even more incensed. "I have had quite enough of the timidity, wrongheadedness and moral relativism that characterizes so much of the commentary of contemporary black elites on the racial issues of our day," he wrote. "The time has come to break ranks with them. These elites are caught in a 'loyalty trap.' They are fearful of engaging in a candid, critical appraisal of the condition of our people because they do not want to appear to be disloyal to the race." And "this rhetorical reticence," he said, "has serious negative consequences for the ability of blacks as a group to grapple with the real problems that confront us. Moreover, it represents a failure of nerve in the face of adversity that may be more accurately characterized as intellectual treason than racial fealty. After all, what more important obligation can the privileged class of black elites have than to tell the truth to their own people?"[20]

Loury wanted more black elites to "break ranks" and do the right thing, but going against the grain can be costly, both personally and professionally. Some of these dissident thinkers—including Thomas, Steele, and Williams—would take the heat and stay the course over the decades, as did

Sowell. Others, such as Loury, have had an on-again, off-again relationship with movement conservatism. And then there are those who later changed their tune or became less vocal than they once were on race-related issues. Perhaps the ostracism and relentless criticism from black peers finally got to them. Perhaps they didn't like being associated in the media with the political right. Or maybe they had a genuine change in thinking about the best ways to address inequality. Or had said their piece and just wanted to move on to other subjects. The reasons vary from one person and circumstance to another, but most of these individuals worked in academia and wanted to remain there. As college campuses—from students to faculty to administrators—became not only more liberal but more intolerant of contrarian points of view, the cost of being a black intellectual renegade rose appreciably.

"I get really annoyed when I get included in these stories about black conservatives," said Carter, a professor at Yale Law School, in a 1991 interview with *The New Republic*. "I have trouble with this notion of a black conservative" and having the term applied to any black person who "criticizes some aspect, however small, of the civil rights agenda," he added. "Black people alone are labeled on this very small spectrum."[21] At the same time, however, Carter's writings didn't merely criticize specific policies advocated by the NAACP and other civil rights groups but also rejected the broader push for black intellectual conformity. "The proposition that there is a right way and a wrong way to be black, and its logical corollary, that people who are black the wrong way are part of the problem rather than part of the solution, recalls the rhetoric of the 1960s and early 1970s, when the idea that one should be a black person of the right kind held a great deal of currency," he wrote. Moreover, "unless one supposes that biology implies ideology, this movement to make race a proxy for views surely involves a category mistake."[22]

John McWhorter, professor of humanities at Columbia University, gained prominence as a black dissident in 2000 after he published *Losing the Race*, a book about cultural barriers to black upward mobility. "Nobody ever believes me when I say this, but I didn't write that as a calling card to the think tank circuit," he told me. "I had no idea anybody was going to pay so much attention. And I think, as you have seen, I was taken up by people who thought I was something that I'm not quite. I'm really in the middle. I'm not a man of the right. I'm really in the middle. And that gradually became clear over the years. I became clearer about it myself over the years."

McWhorter, who has taught at the University of California, Berkeley, as well, and is widely known for his works on language, also addressed the difficulty of living the life of an academic when you hold views that are not progressive and aren't shy about expressing them. "You're part of that community. It's not only school, it's who you know," he said. "It's who is at the parties. It's who your wife introduces you to. It's who lives in your neighborhood. You are unlikely to be somebody who wants to be despised by all those people, and so, you are more likely to go more nuanced." He said that after writing *Losing the Race*, "I remember thinking, I hope that in twenty years I won't have to be one of the people out there saying all these things, getting yelled at and screamed at, et cetera, because there will be a bunch of new people and, hopefully, it will be more mainstream. That has not happened."[23]

The upshot is that black elites on the left only tightened their grip on the prevailing racial narrative, and black conservatism never gained the popularity one might have expected given what was happening in the early 1980s. These outcomes had less to do with the efficacy of the policies the black leaders were pursuing in the name of helping the poor and more to do with their ability to convince the media that other black perspectives were illegitimate, if not harmful. Typical of the view that dominates racial discourse is legal scholar Kimberlé Williams Crenshaw's assertion that "the Black community must develop and maintain a distinct political consciousness," because "the most valuable political asset of the Black community has been its ability to assert a collective identity and to name its collective political reality. Liberal reform discourse must not be allowed to undermine the Black collective identity."[24] For Crenshaw and like-minded others, diversity is fine so long as it's not of the intellectual variety. As the black political scientist Adolph Reed once observed, "the entrenched elites have been able with impunity to identify collective racial interests with an exceedingly narrow class agenda" and present "the illusion of a single racial opinion."[25]

SOWELL FLESHED OUT THE CONCEPTUAL FRAMEWORK FOR his *philosophical* conservatism in books such as *Knowledge and Decisions* and *A Conflict of Visions*. It's an approach rooted in the classical liberal tradition that can be traced to, among others, Edmund Burke, Adam Smith, and Friedrich Hayek, as well as in the empirical methodology exemplified by Milton Friedman and George Stigler's

Chicago school. Sowell's *black* conservatism, by contrast, is less straightforward and more nuanced: "It is hard to think of anyone who is, or has been, a black conservative, in the full sense of the word 'conservative,'" he wrote. "Most of those who are called black conservatives are certainly not interested in preserving the status quo. That status quo includes welfare, failing schools, quotas, and separatism that most black conservatives deplore and attack. Still less are they seeking to return to a status quo ante, such as the Jim Crow era."[26]

Black conservatism today is often equated with an emphasis on self-help, in the mold of nineteenth-century figures such as Frederick Douglass and Booker T. Washington. And Sowell's writings over the decades have shown that groups that confront and address their internal problems are best able to rise socially and economically. "If the history of American ethnic groups shows anything, it is how large a role has been played by attitudes of self-reliance," he wrote. "The success of the antebellum 'free persons of color' compared to the later black immigrants to the North, the advancement of the Italian-Americans beyond the Irish-Americans who had many other advantages, the resilience of the Japanese-Americans despite numerous campaigns of persecution, all emphasize the importance of this factor, however mundane and unfashionable it may be."[27]

For Sowell, however, initiative alone is insufficient. "It would be premature at best and presumptuous at worst to attempt to draw sweeping or definitive conclusions from my personal experiences," he explained. "It would be especially unwarranted to draw Horatio Alger conclusions, that perseverance and/or ability 'win out' despite obstacles. The fact is, I was losing in every way until my life was changed by the Korean War, the draft, and the GI Bill—none of which I can take credit for. I have no false modesty about having seized the opportunity and worked to make it pay off, but there is no way to avoid the fact that there first had to be an opportunity to seize."[28] Government has a role to play in social mobility, albeit a limited one, and incentives matter. The GI Bill's structure, for instance, rewarded people who had already assumed some personal responsibility. To receive financial aid for college, you had to serve in the military, gain admission to an accredited school, and then remain in good academic standing. Government handouts that asked little or nothing of the recipient, and thus risked creating dependency, were the kind that worried Sowell. And he pushed back forcefully at attempts to automatically credit such programs with any black advancement that had occurred:

> It is considered the height of callousness to tell blacks to lift themselves up by their own bootstraps. But the cold historical fact is that most blacks did lift themselves out of poverty by their own bootstraps—before their political rescuers arrived on the scene with civil rights legislation in the 1960s or affirmative action policies in the 1970s.
>
> As of 1940, 87 percent of black families lived below the poverty line. This fell to 47 percent by 1960, without any major federal legislation on civil rights and before the rise and expansion of the welfare state under the Great Society programs of President Lyndon Johnson.

This decline in the poverty rate among blacks continued during the 1960s, dropping from 47 percent to 30 percent. But even this continuation of a trend already begun long before cannot all be attributed automatically to the new government programs. Moreover, the first decade of affirmative action—the 1970s—ended with the poverty rate among black families at 29 percent. Even if that one percent decline was due to affirmative action, it was not much.

The fact that an entirely different picture has been cultivated and spread throughout the media cannot change the historical facts. What it can do—and has done—is make blacks look like passive recipients of government beneficence, causing many whites to wonder why blacks can't advance on their own, like other groups. Worse, it has convinced many blacks themselves that their economic progress depends on government programs in general and affirmative action in particular.[29]

Nevertheless, it is a pragmatic individualism, along with self-help, that defines Sowellian black conservatism. Crenshaw's "collective identity" mindset, which emphasizes group affiliation, is anathema to Sowell, who sees little evidence that embracing a racial or ethnic identity and flaunting it helps underperforming groups excel. "The kind of idealized unity projected by political leaders and intellectuals has seldom existed among any racial or economic minority anywhere," he wrote. "Nor has the economic progress of racial or ethnic groups been much correlated with their closeness to, or remoteness from, such unity." In fact, enforcing racial conformity to advance a particular political or ideological agenda can backfire and fuel more internal division than would have existed in the absence of such efforts. More fundamentally, however, Sowell argued that "the history of ideas—both social and scientific—shows again and again that even the most brilliant thinkers typically grasp only part of the truth, and a fuller understanding comes only after a clash of ideas with others, even when those others are fundamentally mistaken on the whole. Those who insist on a monolithic group ideology are gambling the group's future on being able to achieve such an understanding without this process."[30]

The sociologist Anne Wortham likewise rejects racial cheerleading and stresses individualism as much as, if not more than, black self-reliance. "I am not against Negroes and neither am I for Negroes; and this holds for any other group of people," she said in her 1981 book, *The Other Side of Racism*. "I am for the individual . . . , the self-created person of authentic self-esteem, integrity and honesty, whose individuality is endowed with a free spirit and an active commitment to reason as his only tool of knowledge."[31] For Shelby Steele, a former professor of English, who, like Sowell, left teaching to join the Hoover Institution, it is not the recognition of a racial identity but its prioritization that is the problem. "Both racism, and a lack of development are problems for blacks. We don't have one problem; we have two, and the two are not mutually exclusive. We must struggle on both fronts, individually and collectively," he wrote. "Groups don't learn to read well or open businesses; individuals do. Individuals don't get civil rights legislation passed; groups do."[32] He elaborated on Wortham's view about the primacy of individuality:

Why do we cling to an adversarial, victim-focused identity that preoccupies us with white racism? . . . I think this identity is a weight on blacks because it is built around our collective insecurity rather than our faith in our human capacity to seize opportunity as individuals. It amounts to a self-protective collectivism that obsesses us with black unity instead of individual initiative. To be "black" in this identity, one need only manifest the symbols, postures, and rhetoric of black unity. Not only is personal initiative unnecessary for being "black," but the successful exercise of initiative—working one's way into the middle class, becoming well-off, gaining an important position—may in fact jeopardize one's "blackness," make one somehow less black. The poor black is the true black; the successful black is more marginally black unless he (or she) frequently announces his solidarity with the race in the way politicians declare their patriotism. This sort of identity never works, never translates into the actual uplift of black people. It confuses racial unity with initiative by relying on unity to do what only individual initiative can do. Uplift can only come when many millions of blacks seize the possibilities inside the sphere of their personal lives and use them to take themselves forward. Collectively, we can resist oppression, but racial development will always be, as Ralph Ellison once put it, "the gift of its individuals."[33]

It's noteworthy that black intellectuals such as Steele and Wortham, along with Williams, Thomas, and Woodson, came to their views independent of knowing Sowell or having read him. Williams met him at UCLA in 1969, but by that time the two men were already thinking similarly about racial issues. Upon reading Sowell's *Race and Economics*, Thomas was pleasantly surprised to learn that there were other blacks who shared some of his own views. Wortham told me that her first contact with Sowell was in 1979, after she published an article on black individualism in *Reason* magazine, and he wrote her a letter about it. By that time, she had been writing on the subject for more than ten years. "I didn't know anything about Tom or anybody else—any blacks who thought as I did," she said. "With this letter from him telling me that he had read my article, we began a correspondence from there. I then checked and saw that he had written some things that I had just sort of passed over and hadn't paid attention to." Wortham said she had a similar reaction when she came across Steele's work in the early 1990s: "I was surprised by Shelby, too. I didn't know anything about him. But reading him, just seeing a familiarity between a lot of his analysis and my own, was amazing." The point here is not that these conservatives share the same views on racial or other matters. Rather, what they have in common are beliefs that differ from the liberal orthodoxy. Their experiences demonstrate just how effective those elites and their media allies have been in marginalizing and sometimes suppressing dissenting black scholarship.

ONE OF THE FIRST PLACES WORTHAM PUBLISHED HER work was a lesser-known and now defunct libertarian magazine called *The Freeman*. After reading one of her submissions in the mid-1960s, an editor told her that for him it recalled the writings of George Schuyler, a black journalist who gained prominence in the first half of the twentieth century. Schuyler was a political conservative and fierce anti-Communist who also wrote satirical novels and cultural criticism; he published regularly in H. L. Mencken's influential *American Mercury* magazine. In his history of black conservatism, the author Christopher Alan Bracey wrote that Schuyler's "lifework proves useful in understanding the trajectory of black conservatism in the modern era." Schuyler "lived and died believing that blackness and conservatism were not antithetical, yet he ultimately failed to persuade the masses of black people as to the 'correctness' of his position," said Bracey. "Although Schuyler would lose the ideological battle within his lifetime, his contributions, which provided legitimate warning that liberal approaches to racial empowerment imposed messy and unrealistic expectations on American society, ensured that the legacy of black conservative thought would remain available for resuscitation within black political discourse by future generations of conservatives."[34]

In my discussions about Sowell's legacy with Wortham, Williams, Gerald Early, and others, Schuyler's name came up more often that either Frederick Douglass's or Booker T. Washington's. Indeed, Schuyler's name came up in my conversations with Sowell himself. This was not necessarily because they agreed with the positions that Schuyler took on this issue or that. Rather, it reflected an appreciation of the example he had set in fearlessly challenging, on principle, orthodox thinking on racial matters. Schuyler was an individualist before he was anything else, the black maverick of his day.

In a review of a collection of Schuyler's writings, Sowell called him perhaps "the first black conservative" and "one of the best" besides. "Booker T. Washington may come to mind as a predecessor, but . . . [Washington] was primarily an educator, rather than someone who made his living from his writings, as Schuyler did. Moreover, the circumspection that marked Booker T. Washington's words, during a particularly bitter and dangerous time for black Americans, was nowhere to be seen in Schuyler's later witty, cutting and brutally honest writings that took no prisoners," wrote Sowell. "His insights were always enlightening, even if his conclusions were not always easy to agree with."[35]

Here, Sowell could be describing himself, of course, but even Schuyler was no Thomas Sowell. Schuyler was one of the most prominent black journalists of his day, but by the time he died in 1977, his star had faded, and today his work is largely forgotten. Moreover, even in his prime professional years, which lasted from the 1920s through the 1960s, Schuyler was known almost exclusively for his writings on racial issues. Sowell, by contrast, has a distinguished body of work in social theory and economic history that is entirely separate from his scholarship on race, culture, and inequality. The sheer volume of Sowell's writings is surpassed by few contemporary peers, black or non-black. The breadth and depth of his erudition makes the label "black conservative," however the term is defined, far too limiting. His scholarship will have to be studied and grappled with long after he's gone.

When I asked Gerald Early, a professor of African American studies at Washington University in St. Louis who has followed Sowell's career, why Sowell hadn't received the same recognition as less accomplished scholars, he said it was "because the liberal left dominate intellectual circles. They dominate intellectual circles at universities. They dominate intellectual circles at foundations. They dominate intellectual circles insofar as intellectual prizes and awards are given." Sowell has not sought the approval of these circles, refusing to pull his punches or compromise his principles. And he has paid the price. Still, Early believes that Sowell will get his due sooner or later. "Whether he's given recognition now or it comes after he dies, he will be recognized as a person who has made tremendous contributions and has been an extremely important figure," Early said. "First of all, he's been terrifically prolific. Second, his ideas have been read among a lot of people because of the accessibility of his books. And in the end, he may turn out to be proven right insofar as liberal left public policy hasn't worked."[36]

For his part, Sowell doesn't seem particularly worried about his intellectual legacy. When I asked him where he'd made his mark, he said he'll leave that up to others to determine. "One of the things I admire about John Stuart Mill—despite some things I don't admire—is that he never tried to toot his horn about contributions that he'd made to economics," he said. "And he made some. There were things that hadn't been said by his predecessors. But when he wrote his *Principles of Political Economy*, he just blends it all together. His point is to get across a certain unified body of knowledge and analysis to the reader without bothering to say how much of it came from him, how much from [David] Ricardo, how much from [Adam] Smith and so forth."[37]

Sowell sees his own work, be it on economics, political philosophy, or race, as part of a continuum. "Back in earlier years, you and I were both pretty pessimistic as to whether what we were writing would make any impact—especially since the two of us seemed to be the only ones saying what we were saying," he wrote in a personal letter to his good friend Walter Williams. "Today at least we know that there are lots of other blacks writing and saying similar things—more than I can keep track of, in fact—and many of them are sufficiently younger that we know there will be good people carrying on the fight after we are gone."[38]

ACKNOWLEDGMENTS

FIRST, I THANK MY WIFE, NAOMI, AND OUR CHILDREN for their love and patience. Second, I have been a Senior Fellow at the Manhattan Institute since 2015, and its support has been indispensable. I'm also indebted to the Thomas W. Smith Foundation, the Searle Freedom Trust, the Dian Graves Owen Foundation, and the Bader Family Foundation, whose generosity makes my work possible.

For their assistance with this project, I am also grateful to the following: the Randolph Foundation, the Arthur N. Rupe Foundation, the Gale Foundation, the Charles Koch Foundation, and Harold Grinspoon. Ben Meltzer and Bob Chitester pointed me to old video footage featuring Sowell that I might otherwise have overlooked. Jordan Duecker and Abhay Rangray helped me track down hard-to-find magazine articles and newspaper clips.

Finally, I'd like to acknowledge the individuals who gave me a better understanding of Sowell and his writings: William B. Allen, William R. Allen, William Banks, Fred Barnes, Peter Boettke, Donald Boudreaux, Jennifer Burns, Linda Chavez, John Cogan, Midge Decter, Christopher

Acknowledgments

DeMuth, Gerald Early, Lanny Ebenstein, Erich Eichman, Ross Emmett, Gene Epstein, Richard Epstein, Jason Fertig, George Gilder, Lino Graglia, Dan Hammond, Victor Davis Hanson, Tom Hazlett, David Henderson, Donald Horowitz, Peter Kirsanow, Glenn Loury, Wilfred McClay, John McWhorter, Lawrence Mead, Charles Murray, Michael Novak, Gerald O'Driscoll, Steven Pinker, John Raisian, Gerald Reynolds, Russ Roberts, Peter Robinson, John Sherer, Rita Steele, Shelby Steele, John Taylor, Abigail Thernstrom, Stephan Thernstrom, Richard Vedder, Walter Williams, and Anne Wortham.

NOTES

INTRODUCTION

1. David Isaac, "Live: Thomas Sowell," *The American*, January 1, 2004.

2. Thomas Sowell, *A Personal Odyssey* (Free Press, 2000), xi.

3. Sowell, *Personal Odyssey*, 306.

4. Richard Wright, *Black Boy* (Library of America, 1991), 237.

5. Interview with author, May 20, 2016.

6. Interview with author, April 4, 2016.

7. Thomas Sowell, *A Man of Letters* (Encounter Books, 2007), 102.

8. Sowell, *Man of Letters*, 139.

9. Interview with author, February 20, 2019.

10. Interview with author, December 29, 2015.

11. Sowell, *Personal Odyssey*, 305–306.

12. Thomas Sowell, *Knowledge and Decisions* (Basic Books, 1980), 321.

13. Thomas Sowell, *The Thomas Sowell Reader* (Basic Books, 2011), vii–viii.

CHAPTER I: CHICAGO-SCHOOLED

1. Paul Baran, *Political Economy of Growth* (Monthly Review Press, 1957), 249.

2. Baran, *Political Economy of Growth*, 261.

3. H. Kitamura, "Foreign Trade Problems in Planned Economic Development," in *Economic Development with Special Reference to East Asia*, ed. Kenneth Berril (Palgrave Macmillan, 1964), 202.

4. Gunnar Myrdal, *An International Economy* (Routledge and Kegan Paul, 1956), 201.

5. Peter Bauer, "The Disregard of Reality," *Cato Journal* 7, no. 1 (Spring/Summer 1987): 31.

6. P. T. Bauer, *Equality, the Third World, and Economic Delusion* (Harvard University Press, 1981), 70.

7. P. T. Bauer, "Development Economics: Intellectual Barbarism," in *Economics and Social Institutions: Insights from the Conferences on Analysis and Ideology*, ed. Karl Brunner (Springer, 1979), 51.

8. "A Voice for the Poor," *The Economist*, May 4, 2002.

9. "Reflections on Peter Bauer's Contributions to Development Economics," *Cato Journal* 25, no. 3 (Fall 2005): 441–444.

10. Peter Brimelow, "A Man Alone," *Forbes*, August 24, 1987, 40.

11. Melvin W. Reder, "Chicago Economics: Permanence and Change," *Journal of Economic Literature* 20, no. 1 (March 1982): 19.

12. Thomas Sowell, *A Personal Odyssey* (Free Press, 2000), 122.

13. Thomas Sowell, *Black Education: Myths and Tragedies* (David McKay, 1972), 46.

14. Sowell, *Black Education*, 45.

15. Sowell, *Black Education*, 37.

16. Interview with author, July 5, 2019.

17. Sowell, *Black Education*, 49.

18. Sowell, *Personal Odyssey*, 60.

19. Interview with author, December 29, 2015.

20. Thomas Sowell, *Marxism: Philosophy and Economics* (Quill, 1985), 218.

21. "Q&A with Thomas Sowell," Brian Lamb, host, C-SPAN, April 6, 2005, www.c-span.org/video/transcript/?id=7961.

22. Interview with author, December 29, 2015.

23. Todd G. Buchholz, *New Ideas from Dead Economists: An Introduction to Modern Economic Thought* (Plume, 1999), 241.

24. Thomas Sowell, "Milton Friedman Had Both Genius and Common Sense," *Wall Street Journal*, November 18, 2006.

25. Interview with author, August 1, 2018.

26. George J. Stigler, *The Economist as Preacher and Other Essays* (University of Chicago Press, 1982), 61.

27. J. Daniel Hammond, "The Development of Post-War Chicago Price Theory," *The Elgar Companion to the Chicago School of Economics*, ed. Ross B. Emmett (Edward Elgar, 2010), 10.

28. Gary S. Becker, "Milton Friedman," in *Remembering the University of Chicago: Teachers, Scientists, and Scholars*, ed. Edward Shils (University of Chicago Press, 1991), 142.

29. J. Daniel Hammond, "An Interview with Milton Friedman on Methodology," in *Research in the History of Economic Thought and Methodology*, vol. 10, ed. W. J. Samuels (JAI Press, 1992), 110.

30. Lanny Ebenstein, ed., *The Indispensable Milton Friedman: Essays on Politics and Economics* (Regnery, 2012), 25.

31. Hammond, "Development of Post-War Chicago Price Theory."

32. David R. Henderson, ed., *The Fortune Encyclopedia of Economics* (Warner Books, 1993), 839.

33. Interview with author, December 29, 2015.

34. Thomas Sowell, *Conquests and Cultures: An International History* (Basic Books, 1998), xiv.

35. David M. Levy and Sandra Peart, *Towards an Economics of Natural Equals* (Cambridge University Press, 2020).

36. George J. Stigler, *Memoirs of an Unregulated Economist* (University of Chicago Press, 1988), 27.

37. Ronald H. Coase, "George J. Stigler: An Appreciation," *Regulation*, November/December 1982, 21.

38. Jacob Mincer, "George Stigler's Contributions to Economics," *Scandinavian Journal of Economics* 85, no. 1 (1983): 65–75.

39. Thomas Sowell, *Is Reality Optional? And Other Essays* (Hoover Institution Press, 1993), 71.

40. Thomas Sowell, *A Man of Letters* (Encounter Books, 2007), 235.

41. Thomas Sowell, "A Student's Eye View of George Stigler," *Journal of Political Economy* 101, no. 5 (October 1993): 788.

42. Lanny Ebenstein, *Milton Friedman: A Biography* (Palgrave Macmillan, 2007), 59.

43. Ebenstein, *Milton Friedman: A Biography*, 94.

44. Sowell, quoted in Ebenstein, *Milton Friedman: A Biography*, 91.

45. Lucas, quoted in Ebenstein, *Milton Friedman: A Biography*, 91.

46. Sowell, *Personal Odyssey*, 143.

47. Interview with author, April 1, 2016.

48. Interview with author, March 11, 2016.

49. Stigler, *Unregulated Economist*, 178.

50. Stigler, *Unregulated Economist*, 89.

51. Thomas Sowell, *Intellectuals and Society* (Basic Books, 2011), 543–544.

52. Angela D. Dillard, *Guess Who's Coming to Dinner Now? Multicultural Conservatism in America* (New York University Press, 2001), 1; Jerry G. Watts, "The Case of a Black Conservative: Thomas Sowell: Talent and Tragedy," *Dissent* 29, no. 2 (1982): 301–313.

53. Thomas Sowell, "Milton Friedman's Centenary," *Jewish World Review*, August 1, 2012, http://jewishworldreview.com/cols/sowell080112.php3#.X9GHINhKjIU.

54. Craig Freedman, "Do Great Economists Make Great Teachers? George Stigler as a Dissertations Supervisor," *Journal of Economic Education* 34, no. 3 (Summer 2003): 285.

55. "Arnold 'Al' Harberger," interview conducted October 3, 2000, Commanding Heights, PBS, www.pbs.org/wgbh/commandingheights/shared/minitext/int_alharberger.html.

56. Thomas Sowell, *Markets and Minorities* (Basic Books, 1981), viii.

57. Sowell, *Personal Odyssey*, 138.

58. Sowell, *Personal Odyssey*, 111.

59. Sowell, *Man of Letters*, 4.

60. Thomas Sowell, "The Death of Mrs. G.," *National Review*, April 2, 2012, www.nationalreview.com/2012/04/death-mrs-g-thomas-sowell.

61. Sowell, *Personal Odyssey*, 117; Sowell, *Is Reality Optional?*, 182.

62. Sowell, *Man of Letters*, 5.

63. Sowell, *Personal Odyssey*, 131–132.

64. Jason L. Riley, "Classy Economist," *Wall Street Journal*, March 25, 2006.

CHAPTER 2: A MAN ALONE

1. Thomas Sowell, *A Man of Letters* (Encounter Books, 2007), 8.

2. Deborah Toler, "Black Conservatives," *The Public Eye* 7 (1997): 1–30; Manning Marable, "Black Conservatives and Accommodation: Of Thomas Sowell and Others," *Negro History Bulletin* 45, no. 2 (1982): 32–35.

3. Thomas Sowell, *A Personal Odyssey* (Free Press, 2000), 64.

4. Sowell, *Man of Letters*, 4.

5. Sowell, *Man of Letters*, 20, 21.

6. Sowell, *Personal Odyssey*, 140–141.

7. Sowell, *Man of Letters*, 29–30.

8. Sowell, *Man of Letters*, 41–42.

9. Sowell, *Man of Letters*, 44.

10. Sowell, *Man of Letters*, 38–39.

11. Isabel Wilkerson, *The Warmth of Other Suns: The Epic Story of America's Great Migration* (Random House, 2010), 291.

12. See, for example, Stephan Thernstrom and Abigail Thernstrom, *America in Black and White* (Simon and Schuster, 1997), 183–202; Thomas Sowell, *Black Rednecks and White Liberals* (Encounter Books, 2005), 240–243.

13. Jennifer L. Hochschild, *Facing Up to the American Dream: Race, Class and the Soul of a Nation* (Princeton University Press, 1995), 45, 48.

14. Thomas Sowell, letter to the editor, *New York Times*, May 24, 1970.

15. "Black's Bootstrap Philosophy Attracts Reaganites, Repels Liberals," *Washington Post*, December 6, 1980, www.washington post.com/archive/politics/1980/12/06/blacks-bootstrap-philosophy -attracts-reaganites-repels-liberals/1f607c38-5b0d-47a1-8d19 -e62d0ec71c47.

16. Sowell, *Personal Odyssey*, 286.

17. Sowell, *Man of Letters*, 166.

18. Sowell, *Personal Odyssey*, 291–292.

19. Jerry G. Watts, "The Case of a Black Conservative: Thomas Sowell: Talent and Tragedy," *Dissent* 29, no. 2 (1982): 304.

20. Watts, "Case of a Black Conservative," 307.

21. Frederick Douglass, "What the Black Man Wants: Speech of Frederick Douglass at the Annual Meeting of the Massachusetts Anti-Slavery Society at Boston," 1865, University of Rochester Frederick Douglass Project, https://rbscp.lib.rochester.edu/2946.

22. Booker T. Washington, *Up from Slavery: An Autobiography* (Doubleday, 1951), 223, 224.

23. W. E. B. Du Bois, *The Souls of Black Folk* (Gramercy Books, 1994), 53.

24. W. E. B. Du Bois, *The Philadelphia Negro* (Shocken Books, 1967), 395.

CHAPTER 3: HIGHER EDUCATION, LOWER EXPECTATIONS

1. Thomas Sowell, *A Man of Letters* (Encounter Books, 2007), 65.

2. Thomas Sowell, *A Personal Odyssey* (Free Press, 2000), 153.

3. Thomas Sowell, *Black Education: Myths and Tragedies* (David McKay, 1972), 123.

4. Sowell, *Person Odyssey*, 307.

5. Daniel Patrick Moynihan, *The Negro Family: The Case for National Action* (Office of Policy Planning and Research, US Department of Labor, 1965).

6. Christopher Jencks and David Riesman, "The American Negro College," *Harvard Educational Review* 37, no. 1 (1967): 3–60.

7. Interview with author, December 29, 2015.

8. Interview with author, December 29, 2015.

9. E. Franklin Frazier, *Black Bourgeoisie* (Free Press, 1957), 1–2.

10. Sowell, *Man of Letters*, 102.

11. Thomas Sowell, "Booknotes: Preferential Policies," C-SPAN interview, May 24, 1990, www.c-span.org/video/?12648-1/preferential-policies.

12. Thomas Sowell, *Civil Rights: Rhetoric or Reality?* (Quill, 1984), 7.

13. Sowell, *Personal Odyssey*, 307–308.

14. Nathan Glazer, *Affirmative Discrimination: Ethnic Inequality and Public Policy* (Harvard University Press, 1987), 197.

15. Derrick A. Bell, "Black Students in White Law Schools: The Ordeal and the Opportunity," *University of Toledo Law Review* (Spring-Summer 1970): 552.

16. Jerry G. Watts, "The Case of a Black Conservative: Thomas Sowell: Talent and Tragedy," *Dissent* 29, no. 2 (1982): 306.

17. Clarence Thomas, *My Grandfather's Son* (Harper, 2007), 86–87.

18. Thomas Sowell, *Education: Assumptions Versus History* (Hoover Institution Press, 1986), 125.

19. Randall Kennedy, *For Discrimination: Race, Affirmative Action, and the Law* (Pantheon Books, 2013), 7, 8.

20. John McWhorter, *Losing the Race: Self-Sabotage in Black America* (Perennial, 2000), 229.

21. Stephen L. Carter, *Reflections of an Affirmative Action Baby* (Basic Books, 1991), 15–16.

22. Sowell, *Personal Odyssey*, 306.

23. Allan Bloom, *Giants and Dwarfs: Essays, 1960–1990* (Simon and Schuster, 1990), 365–387.

24. Allan Bloom, *The Closing of the American Mind: How Higher Education Has Failed Democracy and Impoverished the Souls of Today's Students* (Simon and Schuster, 1987), 314.

25. Bloom, *Closing of the American Mind*, 315.

26. Bloom, *Closing of the American Mind*, 320.

27. Sowell, *Personal Odyssey*, 143.

28. Sowell, *Black Education*, 65.

29. Sowell, *Man of Letters*, 47.

30. Thomas Sowell, *Markets and Minorities* (Basic Books, 1981), vii–viii.

31. "Historically Black Colleges and Universities," Thurgood Marshall College Fund, www.tmcf.org/about-us/member-schools/about-hbcus.

32. Susan T. Hill, "The Traditionally Black Institutions of Higher Education, 1860 to 1982," National Center for Education Statistics, US Department of Education, 1985, https://nces.ed.gov /pubs84/84308.pdf, p. 14.

33. Sowell, *Personal Odyssey*, 159.

34. Sowell, *Man of Letters*, 47–48.

35. Sowell, *Personal Odyssey*, 151.

36. Sowell, *Personal Odyssey*, 170.

37. Sowell, *Personal Odyssey*, 306.

38. Shelby Steele, *Shame: How America's Past Sins Have Polarized Our Country* (Basic Books, 2015), 69.

39. Steele, *Shame*, 78–79.

40. Interview with author, December 29, 2015.

41. Sowell, *Personal Odyssey*, 142.

42. Interview with author, December 29, 2015.

43. Thomas Sowell, "Gary Becker: Economist Explored Discrimination," *Atlanta Journal-Constitution*, May 6, 2014, www .ajc.com/news/opinion/gary-becker-economist-explored-discrimi nation/0uEbGruuv5IyCs8wz5Y9pJ.

44. Conversation with author, December 29, 2015.

45. Sowell, *Education: Assumptions Versus History*, 110–112.

46. Thomas Sowell, "Black Studies: Slogan or Social History?," in *Black Studies: Myth and Realities*, by Martin Kilson, C. Vann Woodward, Kenneth B. Clark, Thomas Sowell, Roy Wilkins, Andrew F. Brimmer, and Norman Hill, with an introduction by Bayard Rustin (A. Philip Randolph Educational Fund, 1969), 35.

47. Sowell, "Black Studies," 35.

48. Sowell, "Black Studies," 36, 37.

49. Sowell, *Man of Letters*, 104–105.

50. Sowell, *Black Education*, 69.

51. Sowell, *Man of Letters*, 66.

52. Thomas Sowell, "The Day Cornell Died," *Weekly Standard*, May 3, 1999, reprinted at the Hoover Institution, www.hoover .org/research/day-cornell-died.

53. Sowell, *Man of Letters*, 105.

54. Sowell, *Man of Letters*, 107.

55. Sowell, *Man of Letters*, 66–67.

56. Sowell, *Black Education*, 80.

57. Sowell, "The Day Cornell Died."

58. Sowell, *Black Education*, 81.

59. Sowell, *Personal Odyssey*, 192.

60. Sowell, *Black Education*, 88.

61. Sowell, *Personal Odyssey*, 197.

62. Tevi Troy, "Cornell's Straight Flush," *City Journal*, December 13, 2009, www.city-journal.org/html/cornell%E2%80%99s -straight-flush-10659.html.

63. Sowell, *Black Education*, 95.

64. Thomas Sowell, "New Light on Black I.Q.," *New York Times Magazine*, March 27, 1977. See also Thomas Sowell, "Black Excellence: The Case of Dunbar High School," *The Public Interest*, Spring 1974.

65. Interview with author, December 29, 2015.

66. Interview with author, June 7, 2017.

CHAPTER 4: SOWELL'S RECONSIDERATIONS

1. Thomas Sowell, *Classical Economics Reconsidered* (Princeton University Press, 1974), vii.

2. Interview with author, December 29, 2015.

3. Interview with author, December 29, 2015.

4. Interview with author, December 29, 2015.

5. Thomas Sowell, "Some Thoughts About Writing," *Hoover Digest*, April 27, 2001.

6. Thomas Sowell, *A Personal Odyssey* (Free Press, 2000), 120.

7. Sowell, *Personal Odyssey*, 79.

8. Interview with author, December 29, 2015.

9. Thomas Sowell, *A Man of Letters* (Encounter Books, 2007), 36.

10. Henry Allen, "Hot Disputes," *Washington Post*, October 1, 1981.

11. Sowell, *Classical Economics Reconsidered*, 42.

12. Sowell, *Classical Economics Reconsidered*, 8.

13. Sowell, *Classical Economics Reconsidered*, 14.

14. Sowell, *Classical Economics Reconsidered*, 32.

15. Henry W. Spiegel, review of *Say's Law: An Historical Analysis*, by Thomas Sowell, *Journal of Economic Literature* 11, no. 2 (June 1973): 537–538.

16. Dean A. Worcester Jr., "For Perspective in Feverish Times," *Monthly Labor Review* 97, no. 6 (June 1974): 81–82.

17. Sowell, *Classical Economics Reconsidered*, 106–107.

18. Thomas Sowell, *The Thomas Sowell Reader* (Basic Books, 2011), vii.

19. Mark Blaug, review of *Classical Economics Reconsidered*, by Thomas Sowell, *American Political Science Review* 71, no. 2 (June 1977): 667–668; D. P. O'Brien, review of *Classical Economics Reconsidered*, by Thomas Sowell, *Economica*, n.s., vol. 42, no. 168 (November 1975): 453–454.

20. John Eatwell, Murray Milgate, and Peter Newman, eds., *The New Palgrave: A Dictionary of Economics*, vol. 4 (Palgrave Macmillan, 1987), 249–251, 498–499.

21. James McPherson, "Revisionist Historians," *Perspectives on History*, September 1, 2003, www.historians.org/publications -and-directories/perspectives-on-history/september-2003/revision ist-historians.

22. Jason Riley, "Classy Economist," *Wall Street Journal*, March 25, 2006.

23. Clarence Thomas, *My Grandfather's Son: A Memoir* (Harper, 2007), 105–106.

24. Interview with author, May 20, 2016.

25. Thomas Sowell, "Black Excellence—The Case of Dunbar High School," *Public Interest* (Spring 1974): 3.

26. Sowell, *Man of Letters*, 129.

27. Sowell, *Personal Odyssey*, 241–242.

28. Arthur R. Jensen, "How Much Can We Boost I.Q. Scores and Scholastic Achievement?," *Harvard Educational Review* 39, no. 1 (Winter 1969): 1–123.

29. Sowell, *Man of Letters*, 102.

30. Interview with author, February 20, 2019.

31. Thomas Sowell, "Race and I.Q. Reconsidered," in *Essays and Data on American Ethnic Groups*, ed. Thomas Sowell (Urban Institute, 1978).

32. "An IQ Study of Black Children in White Homes," *New York Times*, April 18, 1976, www.nytimes.com/1976/04/18/archives/an-iq-study-of-black-children-in-white-homes.html; Richard A. Weinberg, Sandra Scarr, and Irwin D. Waldman, "The Minnesota Transracial Adoption Study: A Follow-up of IQ Test Performance at Adolescence," *Intelligence* 16 (1992): 117–135, https://faktasiden.no/dokumenter/minnesota-transracial-adoption-study.pdf.

33. Thomas W. Hazlett and Manuel Klausner, "Interview with Thomas Sowell," *Reason*, December 1980, https://reason.com/1980/12/01/interview-with-thomas-sowell.

34. Sowell, "Race and I.Q. Reconsidered," 231.

35. Thomas Sowell, "New Light on Black I.Q.," *New York Times Magazine*, March 27, 1977.

36. Sowell, "New Light on Black I.Q."

37. William T. Dickens and James R. Flynn, "Black Americans Reduce the Racial IQ Gap: Evidence from Standardization Samples," *Psychological Science* 17, no. 10 (2006): 913–920.

38. Interview with author, 2015.

39. Thomas Sowell, "Ethnicity and IQ," in *The Bell Curve Wars*, ed. Steven Fraser (Basic Books, 1995), 70–79.

40. Sowell, "Ethnicity and IQ," 76.

41. Sowell, "Ethnicity and IQ," 77.

42. Sowell, *Personal Odyssey*, 277–278.

43. David Harsanyi, "Do No Harm: An Interview with Thomas Sowell," *The Federalist*, January 13, 2015, https://thefederalist.com/2015/01/13/do-no-harm-an-interview-with-thomas-sowell.

44. Thomas Sowell, "Western Advocates of 'Nation-Building' Should Master Recently Deceased Statesman's Legacy of Lessons," *Jewish World Review*, May 25, 2015, http://jewishworldreview.com/cols/sowell032515; Hazlett and Klausner, "Interview with Thomas Sowell."

45. Henry Hazlitt, "An Economist's View of 'Planning,'" *New York Times*, September 24, 1944.

CHAPTER 5: SOWELL'S KNOWLEDGE

1. Thomas Sowell, *Dismantling America* (Basic Books, 2010), 338.

2. Thomas Sowell, *A Personal Odyssey* (Free Press, 2000), 302.

3. Interview with author, December 29, 2015.

4. F. A. Hayek, "The Use of Knowledge in Society," *American Economic Review* 35, no. 4 (September 1945): 519–530.

5. Interview with author, December 29, 2015.

6. Thomas W. Hazlett and Manuel Klausner, "Interview with Thomas Sowell," *Reason*, December 1980, https://reason.com/1980/12/01/interview-with-thomas-sowell, 11.

7. Thomas Sowell, *Knowledge and Decisions* (Basic Books, 1980), 4.

8. Sowell, *Knowledge and Decisions*, 3.

9. Sowell, *Knowledge and Decisions*, 18.

10. Sowell, *Knowledge and Decisions*, 110.

11. Sowell, *Knowledge and Decisions*, 79.

12. Sowell, *Knowledge and Decisions*, 164.

13. Sowell, *Knowledge and Decisions*, 165.

14. Sowell, *Knowledge and Decisions*, 362.

15. Sowell, *Knowledge and Decisions*, 339.

16. Sowell, *Knowledge and Decisions*, 340.

17. Sowell, *Knowledge and Decisions*, 367.

18. Sowell, *Knowledge and Decisions*, 369–370.

19. Sowell, *Knowledge and Decisions*, 370.

20. Sowell, *Knowledge and Decisions*, 371.

21. Sowell, *Knowledge and Decisions*, 383.

22. Interview with author, December 29, 2015.

23. Marc Plattner, "Free Markets," *New York Times*, March 23, 1980.

24. Hazlett and Klausner, "Interview with Thomas Sowell," 11.

25. James M. Buchanan, review of *Knowledge and Decisions*, by Thomas Sowell, *Public Choice* 36, no. 1 (January 1981): 199.

26. Thomas Sowell, *A Man of Letters* (Encounter Books, 2007), 161.

27. F. A. Hayek, "The Best Book on General Economics in Many a Year," review of *Knowledge and Decisions*, by Thomas

Sowell, *Reason*, December 1981, https://reason.com/1981/12/01/the-best-book-on-general-econo.

28. Sowell, *Personal Odyssey*, 270.

29. Thomas Sowell, *Controversial Essays* (Hoover Institution Press, 2002), 298.

30. Interview with author, August 2, 2018.

31. "Thomas Sowell—The Ethnic Flaw," *Tony Brown's Journal*, YouTube, posted January 7, 2018, www.youtube.com/watch?v=GtyEMRXpW8Q.

32. Interview with author, February 24, 2016.

33. *Meet the Press*, September 20, 1981.

34. Sowell, *Man of Letters*, 187.

35. *Free to Choose*, vol. 4, "From Cradle to Grave," Free to Choose Network, 1980, www.freetochoosenetwork.org/programs/free_to_choose/index_80.php?id=from_cradle_to_grave.

36. *Firing Line*, "The Economic Lot of Minorities," November 12, 1981, archived at Hoover Institution, https://digitalcollections.hoover.org/objects/6660/the-economic-lot-of-minorities?ctx=605bab01-8be8-4777-81d0-13b978c7eee1&idx=1.

37. *Firing Line*, "The Economic Lot of Minorities."

38. Interview with author, January 23, 2019.

39. "Ethnic America: An Exchange. Maimon Schwarzschild, Martin Glaberman, and Thomas Sowell, reply by Christopher Jencks," *New York Review of Books*, June 16, 1983, www.nybooks.com/articles/1983/06/16/ethnic-america-an-exchange.

40. *Firing Line*, "The Economic Lot of Minorities."

41. *Firing Line*, "Ethnic America: An Exchange."

CHAPTER 6: SOWELL'S VISIONS

1. Thomas Sowell, "Stakes Are Too High to Label Children," *Las Vegas Review-Journal*, May 23, 1993, 2C.

2. Interview with author, March 25, 2017.

3. Interview with author, December 29, 2015.

4. Richard A. Epstein, *Overdose: How Excessive Government Regulation Stifles Pharmaceutical Innovation* (Yale University Press, 2006), 15.

5. Thomas Sowell, *The Vision of the Anointed: Self Congratulation as a Basis for Social Policy* (Basic Books, 1995), 113.

6. "Text of Edward Kennedy's Tribute to His Brother in Cathedral," *New York Times*, June 9, 1968, 56; Bernard Shaw, *The Intelligent Woman's Guide to Socialism and Capitalism* (Brentano's, 1928), 127.

7. William Godwin, *Enquiry Concerning Political Justice*, vol. 2 (University of Toronto Press, 1969), 57.

8. William Godwin, *Enquiry Concerning Political Justice*, vol. 1 (University of Toronto Press, 1969), 161, 162.

9. Thomas Sowell, *The Quest for Cosmic Justice* (Free Press, 1999), 29–30.

10. Thomas Sowell, *A Conflict of Visions: Ideological Origins of Political Struggles*, rev. ed. (Basic Books, 2007), 25–26.

11. Sowell, *Conflict of Visions*, 31, 32.

12. Interview with author, February 25, 2019.

13. Interview with author, February 25, 2019.

14. Sowell, *Conflict of Visions*, 214.

15. Steven Pinker, *The Blank Slate: The Modern Denial of Human Nature* (Penguin, 2002), 291.

16. Interview with author, May 25, 2017.

17. Sowell, *Conflict of Visions*, 88.

18. "A Source of Ideas," *Wall Street Journal*, September 13, 1991, A10.

19. Sowell, *Conflict of Visions*, 59.

20. Interview with author, May 16, 2016. He was referring to Thomas Sowell, *The Thomas Sowell Reader* (Basic Books, 2011), 81–84, 205–208.

21. Interview with author, August 1, 2018.

CHAPTER 7: CIVIL RIGHTS AND WRONGS

1. Richard Fulmer, "The Wit and Wisdom of Thomas Sowell," Ricochet, October 23, 2015, https://ricochet.com/289584/archives/the-wit-and-wisdom-of-thomas-sowell.

2. William M. Banks, *Black Intellectuals: Race and Responsibility in American Life* (W. W. Norton, 1996), 100.

3. G. Franklin Edwards, ed., *E. Franklin Frazier on Race Relations* (University of Chicago Press, 1968), 270.

4. Edwards, *E. Franklin Frazier on Race Relations*, 274, 275.

5. E. F. Frazier, "Is the Negro Family a Unique Sociological Unit?" *Opportunity* 4 (1926): 210.

6. Edwards, *E. Franklin Frazier on Race Relations*, 274.

7. Thomas Sowell, "Booknotes: Preferential Policies," C-SPAN interview, May 24, 1990, www.c-span.org/video/?12648-1/prefer ential-policies.

8. Thomas Sowell, *Civil Rights: Rhetoric or Reality?* (Quill, 1984), 19–20.

9. Sowell, *Civil Rights*, 47.

10. Sowell, *Civil Rights*, 30.

11. Sowell, *Civil Rights*, 31.

12. Sowell, *Civil Rights*, 32.

13. Sowell, *Civil Rights*, 32.

14. Thomas Sowell, *A Man of Letters* (Encounter Books, 2007), 213.

15. Sowell, *Civil Rights*, 84.

16. Sowell, *Civil Rights*, 138–139.

17. Jason L. Riley, *False Black Power?* (Templeton Press, 2017), 47, 67.

18. Thomas Sowell, *Barbarians Inside the Gates and Other Controversial Essays* (Hoover Institution Press, 1999), 261.

19. Sowell, *Civil Rights*, 139–140.

20. Sowell, *Man of Letters*, 207.

21. Thomas Sowell, "Groundbreaking Economist Gets His Due," *Las Vegas Review-Journal*, November 1, 1992.

22. Gary S. Becker and Guity Nashat Becker, *The Economics of Life: From Baseball to Affirmative Action to Immigration, How Real-World Issues Affect Our Everyday Life* (McGraw-Hill, 1997), 125.

23. Thomas Sowell, *Race and Economics* (David McKay, 1975), 159.

24. Thomas Sowell, *The Economics and Politics of Race: An International Perspective* (William Morrow, 1983), 136.

25. Sowell, *Economics and Politics of Race*, 170–171.

26. Jason L. Riley, "A Reality Check on 'Racism' and Urban Decay," *Wall Street Journal*, July 31, 2019.

27. Jason L. Riley, "Good Policing Saves Black Lives," *Wall Street Journal*, June 2, 2020.

28. Nathan Irvin Huggins, "Ethnic Americans," *Yale Review* 72, no. 1 (October 1982): 84–94.

29. Interview with author, March 11, 2016.

30. Mark Helprin, "In Praise of Thomas Sowell," *Claremont Review of Books*, Summer 2017, https://claremontreviewofbooks .com/in-praise-of-thomas-sowell.

CHAPTER 8: CULTURE MATTERS

1. Thomas Sowell, *Black Rednecks and White Liberals* (Encounter Books, 2005), 264.

2. Irving Kristol, "The Negro Today Is Like the Immigrant Yesterday," *New York Times Magazine*, September 11, 1966, 51.

3. Interview with author, March 2006.

4. Thomas Sowell, *A Man of Letters* (Encounter Books, 2007), 268–269.

5. Thomas Sowell, *Wealth, Poverty and Politics: An International Perspective*, rev. ed. (Basic Books, 2016), 427.

6. Thomas Sowell, *The Thomas Sowell Reader* (Basic Books, 2011), 401.

7. Thomas Sowell, "Culture and Equality," Hoover Institution, October 30, 1998, www.hoover.org/research/culture-and-equality.

8. Sowell, *Black Rednecks and White Liberals*, 263.

9. Thomas Sowell, "Booknotes: Preferential Policies," C-SPAN interview, May 24, 1990, www.c-span.org/video/?12648-1/prefer ential-policies.

10. Thomas Sowell, "Conquests and Cultures," C-SPAN, May 21, 1998, www.c-span.org/video/?106136-1/conquests-cultures.

11. Thomas Sowell, *Race and Culture: A World View* (Basic Books, 1994), x.

12. Thomas Sowell, *Conquests and Cultures: An International History* (Basic Books, 1998), 254–255.

13. Sowell, *Race and Culture*, 226.

14. Sowell, *Race and Culture*, 229.

15. Thomas Sowell, "Discrimination, Economics, and Culture," in *Beyond the Color Line: New Perspectives on Race and Ethnicity in America*, ed. Abigail Thernstrom and Stephan Thernstrom (Hoover Institution Press and Manhattan Institute, 2002), 169.

16. Interview with author, June 7, 2017.

17. Sowell, *Race and Culture*, xii–xiii.

18. Thomas W. Hazlett and Manuel Klausner, "Interview with Thomas Sowell," *Reason*, December 1980, https://reason.com/1980/12/01/interview-with-thomas-sowell.

19. Sowell, *Man of Letters*, 213.

20. Sowell, *Man of Letters*, 97–98.

21. Thomas Sowell, *A Personal Odyssey* (Free Press, 2000), 247–248.

22. Thomas Sowell, *Preferential Policies: An International Perspective* (Quill, 1990), 5.

23. Thomas Sowell, *Affirmative Action Around the World: An Empirical Study* (Yale University Press, 2004), 163–164.

24. Wilfred M. McClay, "How the New York Times Is Distorting American History," *Commentary*, October 2019, www.commentarymagazine.com/articles/wilfred-mcclay/how-the-new-york-times-is-distorting-american-history.

25. "Read Ta-Nehisi Coates's Testimony on Reparations," *The Atlantic*, June 19, 2019, www.theatlantic.com/politics/archive/2019/06/ta-nehisi-coates-testimony-house-reparations-hr-40/592042.

26. Sowell, *Preferential Policies*, 148–149.

27. Alphonso Pinkney, *The Myth of Black Progress* (Cambridge University Press, 1984), 17.

28. Thomas Sowell, *Barbarians Inside the Gates and Other Controversial Essays* (Hoover Institution Press, 1999), 257.

29. Thomas Sowell, *Ethnic America: A History* (Basic Books, 1981), 295.

30. Sowell, *Black Rednecks and Black Liberals*, 284.

31. Interview with author, December 29, 2015. The Milton Friedman work he was referring to was "The Methodology of Positive Economics," in *The Essence of Friedman*, ed. Kurt R. Leube (Hoover Institution Press, 1987), 153–184.

32. Interview with author, February 20, 2019.

33. Thomas D. Boston, *Race, Class and Conservatism* (Unwin Hyman, 1988).

34. Interview with author, May 18, 2016.

35. Interview with author, December 18, 2015.

36. Interview with author, January 4, 2016.

37. Quoted in Walter E. Williams, *Up From the Projects: An Autobiography* (Hoover Institution Press, 2010), 115–116.

38. Interview with author, February 20, 2019.

CHAPTER 9: SOWELL MAN

1. Thomas Sowell, "Random Thoughts," *Jewish World Review*, April 29, 2002, www.jewishworldreview.com/cols/sowell0 42902.asp.

2. "Thomas Sowell," interview on *Charlie Rose*, PBS, September 15, 1995, https://charlierose.com/videos/16711.

3. Thomas Sowell, "Booknotes: Preferential Policies," C-SPAN interview, May 24, 1990, www.c-span.org/video/?12648-1/prefer ential-policies.

4. William J. Raspberry, "Civil Rights Gains Bypassing Poorest Negroes," *Washington Post*, October 31, 1965, quoted in Robert L. Woodson Sr., *The Triumphs of Joseph: How Today's Community Leaders Are Reviving Our Streets and Neighborhoods* (Free Press, 1998), 17.

5. Jason L. Riley, "A Black Conservative's War on Poverty," *Wall Street Journal*, April 19, 2014.

6. Woodson, *Triumphs of Joseph*, 19.

7. Woodson, *Triumphs of Joseph*, 20.

8. G. Franklin Edwards, ed., *E. Franklin Frazier on Race Relations* (University of Chicago Press, 1968), 278.

9. Thomas Sowell, *A Man of Letters* (Encounter Books, 2007), 170.

10. Sowell, *Man of Letters*, 170–171

11. Sowell, *Man of Letters*, 174–175.

12. Thomas Sowell, *A Personal Odyssey* (Free Press, 2000), 290.

13. Randall L. Kennedy, "Racial Critiques of Legal Academia," *Harvard Law Review* 102 (June 1989): 1809.

14. Kennedy, "Racial Critiques," 1812.

15. Kennedy, "Racial Critiques," 1812.

16. Charles Willie, *Cast and Class Controversy on Race and Poverty: Round Two of the Willie/Wilson Debate* (General Hall, 1989), 16–17.

17. Thomas D. Boston, *Race, Class and Conservatism* (Unwin Hyman, 1988), 8.

18. *The Fairmont Papers: Black Alternatives Conference* (Institute for Contemporary Studies, 1981), 5.

19. Orlando Patterson, *Ethnic Chauvinism* (Stein and Day, 1977), 155–156.

20. Glenn C. Loury, *One by One from the Inside Out: Essays and Reviews on Race and Responsibility in America* (Free Press, 1995), 190.

21. Fred Barnes, "The Minority Minority," *New Republic*, September 30, 1991.

22. Stephen L. Carter, *Reflections of an Affirmative Action Baby* (Basic Books, 1991), 36, 40.

23. Interview with author, March 30, 2016.

24. Kimberlé Williams Crenshaw, "Race, Reform, and Retrenchment: Transformation and Legitimation in Antidiscrimination Law," *Harvard Law Review* 101, no. 7 (May 1988): 1336.

25. Quoted in Glenn Loury, *One by One*, 191.

26. Thomas Sowell, "The First 'Black Conservative'?," *National Review*, August 20, 2001.

27. Thomas Sowell, *Race and Economics* (David McKay, 1975), 238.

28. Thomas Sowell, *Black Education: Myths and Tragedies* (David McKay, 1972).

29. Thomas Sowell, *Controversial Essays* (Hoover Institution Press, 2002), 65–66.

30. Thomas Sowell, *Race and Culture: A World View* (Basic Books, 1994), 147.

31. Anne Wortham, *The Other Side of Racism* (Ohio State University Press, 1981), xii.

32. Shelby Steele, "Shelby Steele Replies," *Dissent* (Fall 1990): 522.

33. Shelby Steele, *The Content of Our Character* (Harper Perennial, 1991), 170–171.

34. Christopher Alan Bracey, *Saviors or Sellouts: The Promise and Peril of Black Conservatism from Booker T. Washington to Condoleezza Rice* (Beacon Press, 2008), 81–82.

35. Sowell, "The First 'Black Conservative'?," 45–46.

36. Interview with author, February 24, 2016.

37. Interview with author, December 29, 2015.

38. Sowell, *Man of Letters*, 338–339.

INDEX

JULIE BRIMBERG

JASON L. RILEY is a Senior Fellow at the Manhattan Institute and a columnist for the *Wall Street Journal*. He is the author of several previous books, including *Please Stop Helping Us: How Liberals Make It Harder for Blacks to Succeed*.